THEORIES OF INTERNATIONAL POLITICS AND ZOMBIES

THEORIES OF INTERNATIONAL POLITICS AND ZOMBIES

REVIVED EDITION

DANIEL W. DREZNER

PRINCETON UNIVERSITY PRESS

PRINCETON AND OXFORD

Copyright © 2015 by Princeton University Press
Published by Princeton University Press, 41 William Street,
Princeton, New Jersey 08540

In the United Kingdom: Princeton University Press, 6 Oxford
Street, Woodstock, Oxfordshire OX20 1TW

press.princeton.edu

Library of Congress Cataloging-in-Publication Data

Drezner, Daniel W.
    Theories of international politics and zombies / Daniel W.
Drezner.—Revived edition.
        pages cm.
    Includes bibliographical references and index.
    ISBN 978-0-691-16370-3 (pbk. : alk. paper)   1. International
relations—Philosophy.   2. Zombies.   I. Title.
    JZ1305.D74 2014
    327.101—dc23
        2014011052

British Library Cataloging-in-Publication Data is available

This book has been composed in Janson Text
Printed on acid-free paper. ∞
Printed in the United States of America
10 9 8 7 6 5

For my son Sam, who thought this was "way cooler" than my other books; and my daughter Lauren, for reassuring me that "there are no zombies in this land."

CONTENTS

PREFACE

Fifteen years ago, on a cross-country drive, I stopped to visit Graceland. By the time my tour hit the Jungle Room, it was obvious that the thirty-odd people walking through Elvis Presley's mansion fell into two groups. The first contingent was thoroughly, utterly sincere in their devotion to all things Elvis. They were hardcore fans, and Graceland was their Mecca, their Jerusalem, and their Rome. Many of them sounded convinced that the King was still walking the earth. They gasped when they saw the jumpsuit collection, bedazzled by its grandeur.

The second group of tourists was equally delighted to be at Graceland, but for a different reason. These people took great pleasure in the kitschy nature of all things Elvis. To them, a mansion that preserved the aesthetics of green shag carpeting and mirrored walls was both funny and tacky. They too gasped when they saw the jumpsuit collection, bedazzled by how ridiculous they thought it was.

As we ambled along, the sheer professionalism of our tour guide struck me. Her task was not an easy one. She had to provide a veritable font of Elvis knowledge to all of the intense devotees. At the same time, she also had to acknowledge the absurdist nature of the experience for of the rest of the tour group.

With subtle changes in her facial expressions and slight adjustments in her tone of voice, our guide accomplished her task brilliantly. At no point in time did she diminish Elvis in the eyes of his devout followers. Still, I believe all left Graceland that day thoroughly satisfied with their visit.

Think of this book as my tour of a different kind of Graceland, only with a lot more footnotes. Oh—and zombies.

THEORIES OF INTERNATIONAL POLITICS AND ZOMBIES

Thus said the Lord God unto these bones:
Behold, I will cause breath to enter into you,
and ye shall live. And I will lay sinews upon
you, and bring up flesh upon you, and cover
you with skin, and put breath in you, and ye
shall live; and ye shall know that I am the Lord.
So I prophesied as I was commanded; and as
I prophesied, there was a noise, and behold a
commotion, and the bones came together, bone to
its bone. And I beheld, and, lo, there were sinews
upon them, and flesh came up, and skin covered
them above; but there was no breath in them.

—EZEKIEL 37:5–8

INTRODUCTION
. . . TO THE UNDEAD

There are many natural sources of fear in world politics—terrorist attacks, lethal pandemics, natural disasters, climate change, financial panic, nuclear proliferation, ethnic conflict, global cyberwarfare, and so forth. Surveying the cultural zeitgeist, however, it is striking how an unnatural problem has become one of the fastest-growing concerns in international relations. I speak, of course, of zombies.

Whether they are called ghouls, deadites, rotters, walkers, skels, stenches, deadheads, post-humans, the mobile deceased, or the differently animated, the specter of the living dead represents an important puzzle to scholars of international relations and the theories we use to understand the world. What would different theories of international politics predict would happen if the dead began to rise from the grave and feast upon the living? How valid—or how rotten—are these predictions?

Serious readers might dismiss these questions as fanciful, but concerns about flesh-eating ghouls are manifestly evident in popular culture. Whether one

Figure 1. Popular and scholarly interest in zombies.
Sources: Wikipedia, Web of Science.

looks at films, songs, games, or books, the genre is clearly on the rise. As figure 1 shows, the release of zombie films has spiked since the dawn of the new millennium; according to conservative estimates, well more than one-third of all zombie films have been released since the September 11, 2001 terrorist attacks.[1] Figure 2 suggests that these estimates might be understated. According to one recent analysis, zombies have become the most important source of postapocalyptic cinema in recent years.*

---

*Phelan 2009. Zombies are clearly a global cinematic phenomenon. Beyond the United States, there have been Australian, British, Chinese, Czech, German, Irish, Italian, Japanese, Korean, Mexican, and Norwegian zombie flicks. See Russell 2005 for an exhaustive filmography.

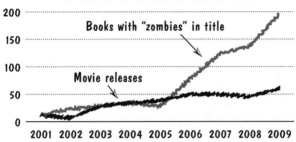

INTEREST IN ZOMBIES SINCE 2000

Figure 2. Interest in zombies since 2000.
Sources: Amazon.com, Wikipedia.

Nor is this interest limited to celluloid. A series of zombie video games, including the Resident Evil and Left 4 Dead franchises, served as a precursor for the renaissance of zombie cinema. These have been followed up by even more video games, including Plants vs. Zombies and The Last of Us. The undead have spread to television in recent years, including Comedy Central's *Ugly Americans* (2010–12), MTV's *Death Valley* (2011–12), BBC America's *In the Flesh* (2013–), and the CW's *iZombie* (2014–), as well as AMC's ratings powerhouse *The Walking Dead* (2010–). Indeed, in 2013, *The Walking Dead* beat all other shows in its time slot in the ratings—including *Sunday Night Football*. Zombies have also seeped onto the written page. The popular literature ranges from how-to survival manuals,[2] to children's books,[3] to revisionist early Victorian novels to prestigious fiction.[4] Comic book series

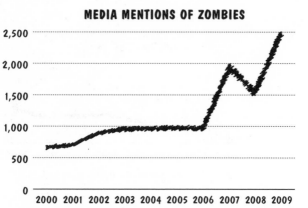

Figure 3. Media mentions of zombies. Source: Lexis-Nexis.

such as The Walking Dead and Marvel Zombies have spread rapidly over the past ten years. One book editor gleefully told *USA Today* that "in the world of traditional horror, nothing is more popular right now than zombies. The living dead are here to stay."[5] A cursory scan of newspaper databases shows a steady increase in posthuman mentions (see figure 3). Clearly the living dead have lurched from marginal to mainstream.

One could dismiss the zombie trend as merely feeding a mass public that craves the strange and bizarre. Such an explanation would be only skin-deep. Popular culture often provides a window into the subliminal or unstated fears of citizens, and zombies are no exception. Some cultural commentators argue that the September 11, 2001, terrorist attacks are a primary cause for renewed interest in the living dead, and the numbers appear to back up this assertion (see figure 2).[6] Certainly the subsequent anthrax attacks in the autumn of 2001 raised fears about bioterrorism and biosecurity.[7] As Peter Dendle notes, "It is clear that the zombie holocausts vividly painted in movies and video games have tapped into a deep-seated anxiety about society."[8] Zombies have been an obvious metaphor for medical maladies, mob rule, and Marxist dialectics.*

Some international relations scholars would posit that interest in zombies is an indirect attempt to get a cognitive grip on what former US secretary of defense Donald Rumsfeld famously referred to as the "unknown unknowns" in international security.[9] Perhaps, however, there also exists a genuine but publicly unacknowledged fear of the dead rising from the grave and feasting upon the entrails of the living. Major universities and police departments have developed "mock" contingency plans for a zombie outbreak.[10] An increasing number of college students are playing Humans versus Zombies on their campuses to relieve stress—or perhaps to prepare for the

---

*In one of the more interesting interpretations, Grady Hendrix (2008) concludes that Juan Carlos Fresnadillo's *28 Weeks Later* (2007) is "an effective metaphor for the unstoppable, global spread of Starbucks." For more general discussions of how zombies are used as metaphors, see Aquilina and Hughes 2006; Christie and Lauro 2011; Comaroff and Comaroff 2002; Cooke 2009, chap. 7; Fay 2008; Harper 2002; Kay 2008; Lauro and Embry 2008; Newitz 2006; Paffenroth 2006; Russell 2005; Smith? 2011; and Webb and Byrnard 2008.

inevitable army of the undead.[11] *Outdoor Life* magazine has run a "Zombie Guns" feature, stressing that "the only way to take 'em out is with a head shot."[12] Clearly, biosecurity is a new imperative among national governments.[13] The government of Haiti has laws on the books to prevent the zombification of individuals.[14] Multiple US government agencies, including the Department of Homeland Security and the Centers for Disease Control and Prevention, have issued public statements with respect to the living dead. US Strategic Command has developed CONPLAN 8888, entitled "Counter-Zombie Dominance." Its very first line reads, "This plan was not actually designed as a joke."[15] One can only speculate what other governments are doing in private. Despite CONPLAN 8888, in 2013, Chairman of the Joint Chiefs of Staff Martin Dempsey went to the Pentagon and explicitly asked his service commanders, "Oh my God, what are we going to do if the zombies attack?"[16]

One must be wary of overstating the case—after all, flesh-eating ghouls are not the only paranormal phenomenon to spark popular interest. In recent years, aliens, ghosts, vampires, wizards, witches, and hobbits have also been on the tip of everyone's tongue. For some, the specter of zombies pales in comparison to other paranormal creatures. The disdain of cultural elites has abetted this perspective by placing zombies in the derivative, low-rent part of the paranormal spectrum—a shuffling, stumbling creature that desires only braaaaiiiiiinnnnnnns. Twenty-five years ago, James Twitchell concluded that "the zombie is an utter cretin, a vampire with a lobotomy."[17] Despite the zombie renaissance in popular culture, these ghouls are still considered disreputable. Paul Waldmann observed in 2009 that "in truth, zombies should be boring . . . what's remarkable is that a villain with such little complexity has thrived for so long."[18] In 2010, the Academy Awards presented a three-minute homage to horror cinema, and only a millisecond was devoted to any zombie film—way less than that Chucky doll. No zombie has the appeal of J. K. Rowling's Harry Potter or the Twilight series' Edward Cullen.

From a public policy perspective, however, zombies merit greater interest than other paranormal phenomenon. As figure 4 demonstrates, a Google Trends analysis demonstrates that interest in zombies has far outpaced interest in other paranormal phenomena—especially the friggin' hobbits. Furthermore, the gap in attention has surged since the 2008 financial crisis. The living dead appear to resonate more than other paranormal actors in an age of uncertainty. Scientists and doctors acknowledge that, in contrast to vampires or demons, some variation of a zombie could exist in our physical world.* Zombies

*Berlinski 2009; Davis 1985, 1988; Efthimiou and Gandhi 2007; Koch and Crick 2001; Littlewood and Douyon 1997. In the main, these possibilities adhere closely to the traditional Haitian notion of the zombie as a human revived via voodoo and devoid

Zombies, in contrast to vampires, do not thrive in high schools.

possess a patina of plausibility that vampires, ghosts, witches, demons, or wizards lack; the creation of a zombie does not necessarily require a supernatural act. Indeed, this plausibility of zombies can be seen in expert surveys. A recent poll of professional philosophers showed that more than 58 percent of philosophers believed that zombies could exist on some level.

---

of free will, rather than the flesh-eating ghouls that started with George Romero's *Night of the Living Dead* (1968).

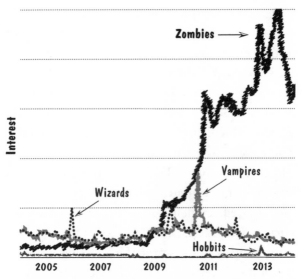

Figure 4. Google Trends analysis of paranormal actors.

In contrast, fewer than 15 percent of the same respondents were prepared to believe in God.* Given the raft of religion and theology departments in the academy, it seems churlish for scholars to neglect the question of reanimated corpses snacking on human flesh.

The traditional narrative of the zombie canon also looks different from stories about other paranormal

*Data from the PhilPapers Survey of 3,226 professional philosophers and others carried out in November 2009 (http://philpapers.org/surveys/). The philosophical definition of *zombie* (a being identical to humans in every way except lacking in consciousness) is somewhat different from the vernacular meaning (a reanimated corpse intent on eating human flesh). There is some conceptual overlap between the two meanings, however. As David Chalmers (1996, 96) puts it, "all is dark inside" for both categories of zombies.

beings. Zombie stories usually end in one of two ways—the elimination/subjugation of all zombies, or the eradication of humanity from the face of the earth.[19] If popular culture is to be believed, the peaceful coexistence of ghouls and humans is a remote possibility. Such extreme all-or-nothing outcomes are less common in the vampire or wizard literatures. There are far fewer narratives of vampires trying to take over the world.[20] Instead, creatures of the night are frequently co-opted into existing power structures. Indeed, recent literary tropes suggest that vampires or wizards can peacefully coexist with ordinary teens in many of the world's high schools, provided they are sufficiently hunky.[21] Zombies, not so much. If it is true that "popular culture *makes* world politics what it currently *is*," then the international relations community needs to digest the problem posed by flesh-eating ghouls in a more urgent manner.[22]

THE ZOMBIE LITERATURE

It would be reckless to proceed with any discussion of the zombie problem without first reviewing the multidisciplinary literature on the subject. Thankfully, the living dead are now the focus of rigorous scholarship, as figure 1 demonstrates. The humanities are replete with cultural decompositions of flesh-eating ghouls.[1] Philosophers have chewed over the conceivability and metaphysical possibility of zombies at some length.[2]

The natural sciences have also started attacking the zombie question. Zoologists have looked at the presence of zombielike creatures elsewhere in the animal kingdom.[3] Biologists have researched the disease-transmission properties of humans biting humans.[4] Forensic anthropologists have considered how long zombies can persist while their body decomposes, and physicians have identified a possible name for the zombie infection: ataxic neurodegenerative satiety deficiency syndrome.[5] Physicists have explored the best place to hide from the "random walk" pattern of zombielike bodies.[6] Computer scientists are working frantically to ward off online zombies, or botnets.[7] Mathematicians have modeled the theoretical spread of zombies, and offered some sobering conclusions: "An outbreak of zombies infecting humans is likely to be disastrous, unless extremely aggressive tactics are employed against the undead. . . . A zombie outbreak is likely to lead to the collapse of civilization, unless it is dealt with quickly."[8] This study has provoked some critical feedback.[9] Additional modeling, however, suggests the deep problems governments will face in coping with individual responses to the spread of the living dead.[10]

This brief survey of the zombie literature reveals an immediate and daunting problem. The humanities and the hard sciences have devoted sustained attention to the problem posed by reanimated corpses feasting upon human flesh. The social sciences, however, are curiously deficient in this line of inquiry. From its founding to 2011, the advisory board for the Zombie Research Society did not contain a single social scientist.[11] When social scientists mention zombies, they usually do so only for metaphorical reasons.[12] While economists have rigorously modeled the optimal macroeconomic policies for a world of vampires, they have only just started to flesh out a zombie consumption function.[13] Despite the mob tendencies of the living dead, sociologists have not analyzed the asocial sociability of zombies. Political science has only just begun to address the policy responses and governance issues associated with the living dead. When compared to work in cognate disciplines, the social sciences in general—and international relations in particular—suffer from a zombie gap.

This dearth of scholarly inquiry should gnaw at international relations scholars and policy makers alike. Classical authors were clearly aware of threats posed by the living dead, as the passage from Ezekiel that opened this book suggests. In *The Art of War*, Sun Tzu stressed the importance of fighting when on "death ground," clearly anticipating the imminent threat posed by the undead. In his *History of the Peloponnesian War*, Thucydides recounted how a "plague that showed itself to be something quite different from ordinary diseases" would lead to general lawlessness and chaos. In the *Arthashastra*, Kautilya specified the need for "experts in the occult" to ward off the spread of unusual diseases. When Thomas Hobbes described the state of nature as one of "continuall feare, and danger of violent death, and the life of man solitary, poore, nasty, brutish, and short," zombies were either on his mind or outside his door.[14]

In contrast, recent scholarship has been either inarticulate or brain-dead on the subject. Modern international relations theorists have eagerly delved into other paranormal phenomena—including UFOs, wizards, hobbits, Cylons, and vampires—but only in recent years has a nascent literature emerged on zombies.[15] It is genuinely surprising that more scholarship in world politics has not been devoted to the living dead.

From a policy-making perspective, further research into flesh-devouring ghouls is also warranted. On the one hand, significant twenty-first century international relations "shocks" such as the 2008 financial crisis, the Arab Spring unrest, and the Russian annexation of Crimea took most governments by surprise. That these were shocks demonstrates the likelihood that even powerful actors are underestimating "black swan" events. In many ways, flesh-eating ghouls are the scariest, ugliest black swan imaginable.

On the other hand, as powerful decision makers have demonstrated in recent years, these low-probability events can also elicit hyperbolic policy responses if the predicted effects are severe.[16] Former vice president Dick Cheney believed that extreme measures were warranted if there was even a 1 percent chance of a severe terrorist attack.[17] If a policy analyst applies this logic to the undead, then preventive measures are clearly necessary. Even if the probability of a zombie uprising is much smaller, the dead rising from the grave and feasting on the living represent a greater existential threat to humanity than does nuclear terrorism. Indeed, the living dead literally embody what Jessica Stern calls a "dreaded risk."[18]

Because the postulated effects of zombies appear to be so dire in film and fiction, more strategic planning should be devoted to this scenario. It is certainly possible that any counterzombie contingency plans will disintegrate at first contact with the undead enemy.[19] Nevertheless, the planning process itself can improve future policy responses, a fact that planners in US Strategic Command have publicly acknowledged.[20] If the record of military incursions in this century teaches us anything, it is the dangers of conducting foreign policy with only a facile or superficial knowledge about possible enemies. Traditional tools of statecraft like nuclear deterrence, economic sanctions, or diplomatic démarches would be of little use against the living dead.* Zombies crave human flesh, not carrots or sticks. More controversial techniques such as torture, enhanced interrogation, drone warfare, or widespread electronic surveillance would also be of little use. The undead do not feel pain, nor are they terribly active on social media networks. A deep knowledge of zombies—and the range of possible policy response to zombies—is required in order to avoid both overreactions and underreactions.

*The use of nuclear weapons—explicitly advocated in US Strategic Command's CONPLAN 8888—would be a catastrophic mistake in a zombie-infested world. Ghouls cannot be deterred, stripping the one useful trait such weapons possess. Nuclear weapons would no doubt incinerate massive numbers of zombies. Unlike human beings, however, the undead would survive any radioactive fallout from the nuclear blast. Indeed, zombies carrying lethal doses of radiation would pose a double threat to humans as they stumbled around: death by radiation, or reanimation by zombie bite. If any government was so foolhardy as to launch a first strike, it would create the only thing worse than an army of the living dead: a mutant, radioactive army of the living dead.

The rising popularity of zombies is in and of itself another reason for further investigation. Research suggests that exposure to paranormal narratives increases the likelihood of individuals to believe in their existence.[21] Such beliefs have a viral quality— that is, exposure to other people's beliefs will increase the likelihood of accepting that same belief, regardless of its logical plausibility.[22] As zombies bleed across all dimensions of popular culture, more people will come to believe, fear, and dread their existence. Fear is a powerful emotion that can profoundly affect policy making across several dimensions.[23] A phobia of the living dead could lead to self-defeating policy responses in the same way that the fears of terrorist attacks led the post-9/11 U.S. military to torture prisoners at Abu Ghraib. Clearly, public fears of being devoured by flesh-eating ghouls can only be allayed by rigorous scholarship.

In many ways, international relations is *the* missing link in most discussions of how to cope with a zombie uprising. The undead menace usually goes global in the zombie canon. These stories lack a basic grounding in world politics, however. Narratives about the living dead use small communities or families as their unit of social analysis. The effect of national governments or international relations is barely discussed —even though logic suggests that the living dead would provoke *some* kind of policy response. As Jonathan Maberry observes, "most of the major entries in the genre have military, police, or civilian defense as part of the backstory."[24] The problem is that these responses are either dismissed or glossed over quickly to get to the apocalyptic portion of the story.[25] Even if official policy responses are suboptimal, they should be factored into our expectations about how the world would respond when the dead walk the earth—and how international relations would look afterward.

What follows is an attempt to satiate the ever-growing hunger for knowledge about the interaction of zombies and world politics. Alas, some lines of academic inquiry are simply not feasible. Institutional review boards and human subjects committees would impose formidable barriers to randomized control trials or other experimental methods. The rare nature of zombie outbreaks make statistical approaches unsuitable. Nevertheless, there are many possible ways to proceed—develop a new theoretical model, interview experienced policy makers about their experiences with zombielike scenarios, create powerful computer simulations, or search for other modalities.

Looking at the state of international relations theory, however, one quickly realizes the absence of consensus about the best way to model world politics. There are multiple existing paradigms that attempt to explain international relations. Each of them has a different take on how zombies affect world politics and how political actors would respond to the living dead. I have therefore decided to flesh out how existing international relations theories would predict what would happen in response to an outbreak of zombies.* What might these theories predict will happen? What policy recommendations will follow from these theories? When will hiding and hoarding be the right idea?

This analysis is useful not merely because of a possible zombie threat but as a way to stress-test our existing theories of international politics. Scholars, commentators, and policy analysts rely on deductive theories as a cognitive guide in a complex world. The more observational implications that flow from these theories the greater their explanatory leverage over known unknowns *and* unknown unknowns.[26] One measure of their explanatory leverage is their ability to offer useful and counterintuitive predictions in the wake of exogenous shocks to the system. Surely an army of the ravenous living dead would qualify as such a shock.

---

*Space constraints prevent a fuller discussion of how some theories—such as Marxism—would cope with flesh-eating ghouls. Indeed, Marxism would appear to have more explanatory leverage in analyzing the traditional Haitian or voodoo zombies. I would ordinarily encourage such paradigms to focus on flesh-eating ghouls, but in this instance I am wary. To be blunt, this project is explicitly prohuman, whereas Marxists would likely sympathize more with the zombies. To Marxist scholars, the undead symbolize the oppressed proletariat and could be welcomed as a vanguard that could finally eliminate the exploitation of the capitalist mode of production.

Zombie denialists might argue that because there is minimal chance of the dead rising from the grave and feasting upon the living this exercise will yield little in the way of enlightenment. This ignores the ways in which world politics is changing and the need for international relations scholarship to change with it. Traditionally, international relations has been concerned with the interactions among nation-states. Many current security concerns, however, center on violent nonstate actors. A growing concern in world politics is the draining of power from purposive actors to the forces of entropy.[27] In the most important ways, flesh-eating ghouls are an exemplar for salient concerns about the global body politic. Zombies are the perfect twenty-first-century threat: they are not well understood by serious analysts, they possess protean capabilities, and the challenges they pose to states are very, very grave.

I will rely on two sources of evidence to buttress the theoretical paradigms. The first data source is the social science literature on events akin to an attack of the undead: pandemics, disasters, bioterrorism, and so forth. Past responses to calamitous events can inform our expectations of how states and nonstate actors would respond to the presence of reanimated and ravenous corpses.

The second data source is the fictional narratives about zombies that exist in popular culture. In recent years, policy makers have relied on the creators of fictional narratives for insights into "out of the box" threat scenarios and outcomes; indeed, US Strategic Command stated explicitly in their counterzombie plan that, "the use of science fiction sources does provide a compelling advantage for military planners."[28] Similarly, international relations scholars have branched out beyond standard statistical analyses and comparative case studies for their empirical analysis. These scholars have used simulations and agent-based modeling to test their theories.[29] The use of fictional narratives as a data source for theory building—particularly horror and science fiction—has also become more common in recent years.[30]

To be sure, there are some dangers in this approach that should be acknowledged at the outset. First, the narratives of film and fiction might be skewed in ways that could bias our analysis.[31] Perhaps people would respond to a real night of the living dead in a different manner than George Romero, Max Brooks, or Robert Kirkman posit. This possibility will be considered—but as we shall see, there is a hidden heterogeneity to the zombie canon. There are a sufficient number of variations to the traditional ghoul narrative to illuminate each of the major international relations paradigms.*

*To sidestep the myriad controversies that plague the community of zombie enthusiasts, my primary empirical focus will be on the major works in the zombie canon: George Romero's films, Max Brooks's novels, Robert Kirkman's comic books and television show, and the most popular works released in recent years.

Second, pursuing a paradigmatic approach to explain the field of international relations has some drawbacks. Some might argue that paradigmatic debates have yielded much more heat than light. The predictive power of these approaches has been underwhelming.[32] Other scholars posit that calling these different theoretical approaches paradigms gives them a coherence and completeness that they normally lack.[33] Some go so far as to suggest that paradigms are unnecessary for the pursuit of scientific inquiry in international politics, that an approach that relies on the building blocks of interests and institutions offers greater analytical leverage.[34]

Nevertheless, these paradigms do help to clarify what different international relations theorists believe is important in world politics. Whether researchers or policy makers admit it or not, all coherent international relations work proceeds from some paradigmatic assumptions. A theoretical attack of the undead can further reveal how these different approaches diverge in their predictions. In eliding some internal theoretical disputes, however, I fully acknowledge that I am committing some conceptual violence to these paradigms. In fairness, however, the undead would likely do far worse.

Before proceeding with the variegated predictions of different international relations theories, a few definitions and distractions must be addressed.

DEFINING A ZOMBIE

Definitions of zombies range from the philosophical one of a human being without consciousness to the anthropological one of a person buried and then resurrected by a conjurer. US Strategic Command offers eight distinct categories of the undead in their counter-zombie plan—including chicken zombies.[1] Consistent with the Zombie Research Society, I choose to treat the zombie as a biologically definable, animated being occupying a human host, with a desire to eat human flesh.[2] This definition is at variance with the etymology of the word *zombie* in West African and Haitian voodoo rituals. Those reanimated corpses, however, do not represent a transnational security threat—indeed, these "traditional" zombies are usually described as the most obedient of laborers. All modern works in the zombie canon are rooted in the kind of ghoul that first appeared in George Romero's *Night of the Living Dead* (1968). Because they can spread across borders and threaten states and civilizations, it is flesh-eating ghouls that should animate the concern of international politics scholars and policy makers.

From a national security perspective, the three relevant assumptions about zombie behavior are as follows:

1. Zombies desire human flesh; they will not eat other zombies . . . because that is just gross.
2. Zombies cannot be killed unless their brain is destroyed.
3. Any human being bitten by a zombie will inevitably become a zombie.

Almost every modern zombie narrative adheres to these rules.[3] These criteria do eliminate some of the ur-narratives that laid the foundation for the zombie canon, such as Richard Matheson's 1954 novel *I Am Legend* or Don Siegel's 1956 film *Invasion of the Body Snatchers*.[4] Nevertheless, any zombies who satisfy these rules would have a pronounced impact upon international relations. In turn, however, the nature of international relations would affect the global response to an attack of flesh-eating ghouls.

DISTRACTING DEBATES ABOUT
FLESH-EATING GHOULS

There is significant variation in zombie capabilities across the canon—and vigorous debate within the zombie studies community over these differences.[1] In most of the literature, zombies cannot talk, and do not retain any attributes of their human identities. There are distinguished exceptions, however, in both film (Dan O'Bannon's *Return of the Living Dead*, 1985; Robert Rodriguez's *Planet Terror*, 2007; Jonathan Levine's *Warm Bodies*, 2013) and fiction.[2] In most of the narratives, only humans can turn into zombies; in the Resident Evil franchise, however, dogs and birds are affected as well. It is usually assumed that there are no gender differences among the walking undead, but recent films provide some unusual exceptions.* The living dead usually are created from a zombie

---

*In Jake West's *Doghouse* (2009), the toxin that creates zombies only affects women. Jay Lee's *Zombie Strippers* (2008) offers the intriguing premise of a virus that turns men into garden-variety ghouls but empowers women into developing a better appreciation of both the philosophy of Friedrich Nietzsche and the complexities of pole dancing.

bite, but in both George Romero's *Night of the Living Dead* (1968) and Robert Kirkman's TV series *The Walking Dead (2010–)*, anyone who dies turns into a flesh-eating ghoul. Whether zombies have desires beyond the consumption of human flesh is unclear. Most narratives do not discuss this question, but the Italian zombie films of the 1980s, as well as Peter Jackson's *Dead Alive* (1992), suggest that ghouls lust after other ghouls. There is no consensus about how long a zombie can exist before decomposing. Obviously, most works assume that a human being needs to die before becoming a zombie—but most scholarship also counts Danny Boyle's *28 Days Later* (2002) and Juan Carlos Fresnadillo's *28 Weeks Later* (2007) to be part of the canon. In those films, the "rage virus" does not exactly kill the infected but rather transforms them into bloodshot, bloodthirsty maniacs in less than thirty seconds.

Surveying the state of the zombie literature, the two sharpest disagreements are about their origins and their capabilities. This provides us, as social scientists, with an excellent means to determine whether zombie-specific variables—their origins and their speed—have a dramatic effect on outcomes in international relations. If the same outcomes persist regardless of variation in these variables, then they are unimportant as causal factors.

The greatest variation in zombie narratives is their origin story: What caused the dead to reanimate and prey upon the living? The reasons provided range from the extraterrestrial to the technological to the microbiological to the supernatural. In Romero's *Night of the Living Dead* it is suggested that a returning space probe contaminated Earth with a heretofore unknown form of radiation. Technology can contribute to the creation of the living dead. Stephen King used a computerized "pulse" in *Cell* (2006).[3] In the Resident Evil franchise, the Umbrella Corporation biologically engineered the "T-virus." Max Brooks attributed the source of zombies to the Solanum virus, which in his 2006 novel *World War Z* has its origins at the bottom of China's Three Gorges Dam reservoir.[4] In Z. A. Recht's novel *Plague of the Dead* (2006), the virus originates in central Africa.[5] Bruce McDonald's *Pontypool* (2009) suggests that the English language is responsible for the creation of zombies. In Jackson's *Dead Alive*, the bite of a Sumatran "rat monkey" creates the first batch of undead. The narrator in Ruben Fleischer's *Zombieland* (2009) offers a simple explanation: "Mad cow became mad person became mad zombie."

Supernatural explanations have also been provided in the literature. In Brian Keene's zombie novels, demonic possession is responsible; Romero's *Dawn of* *the Dead* (1978) provides the most iconic explanation in the canon: "When there's no more room in hell, the dead will walk the earth."* For Michael Jackson, the dead start to walk in their masquerade for the murkiest of reasons: the evil of the "Thriller."

Clearly, there is no consensus on what causes the reanimation of corpses into flesh-eating automatons. For our concerns, this discord is diverting but irrelevant. From a foreign policy/national security perspective, the primary reason to be concerned about the cause of zombies is to adopt preventive measures and policies with which to handle zombie-infested jurisdictions. As antiterrorism and homeland security policies suggest, however, massive investments in prevention cannot be 100 percent foolproof. It only takes one zombie to create an army of the undead.

Unfortunately, the very multiplicity of causal mechanisms makes prevention both highly unlikely and prohibitively expensive.[6] A truly preemptive doctrine would require a comprehensive and draconian list of

---

*It is interesting to note that Romero's explanations have trended in the opposite direction from the rest of the zombie literature. In general, the genre has moved toward scientific and pseudoscientific explanations involving viruses, prions, and toxins. In his films, however, Romero has drifted from the radiation backstory of *Night of the Living Dead* (1968) to a more supernatural explanation. In the later *Day of the Dead* (1985), the character John scoffs at the idea of a scientific explanation, concluding simply, "We've been punished by the Creator. He visited a curse on us, so we might get a look at what Hell was like."

policy measures. It is unlikely that any government would be both willing and able to block all relevant research efforts into biological, nuclear, and computer technology, monitor and prevent any religious interference that could stir up the undead, *and* ward off the evil of the Thriller. Even powerful governments will lack both the foresight and the capabilities to block all of the possible causal mechanisms through which the dead can be resurrected.

This is especially true given that, in most of the origin stories, the emergence of zombies is accidental rather than intentional. The complexity of precautionary measures could *increase* the likelihood of the living dead stalking humankind by increasing the probability of a "normal accident."[7] US efforts to develop countermeasures to bioterrorism, for example, have actually increased the supply of deadly toxins, thus concomitantly increasing the probability of an accident triggering the unintended release of a biotoxin to the outside world.[8] In the case of bioterrorism, however, the federal government could at least point to the existence of prior attacks to validate preventive measures. Without a prior history of zombie attacks for justification, no government could produce a cost-benefit analysis to warrant extensive precautionary policies.

International relations scholarship is less concerned with the *cause* of zombies than their *effect* on world politics. To use the language of social science, flesh-eating ghouls are the *independent variable*. As it turns out, the creators of zombie narratives largely share this position. It is telling that these stories usually provide only perfunctory explanations for how "Zombie Zero" was born. In *Night of the Living Dead*, for example, Romero only provided a causal explanation when pressured by the film's distributors.[9] Multiple commentators have correctly observed the reason for this lack of concern; these stories are always set after the outbreak, as civilization itself is either imperiled or destroyed.[10] Like international relations scholars, the creators of zombie narratives are more interested in how the living dead affect human institutions. The absence of consensus about what causes zombies might be vexing—but, for our purposes, it is not problematic.

An even fiercer doctrinal dispute involves how fast zombies can move.[11] From Romero's *Night of the Living Dead* through Brooks's *World War Z*, the living dead walked, shuffled, lurched, crawled, or stumbled —but they did not run. Recent zombie survival manuals stress this point.[12] Brooks is particularly emphatic, asserting, "Zombies appear to be incapable of running. The fastest have been observed to move at the rate of barely one step per 1.5 seconds. . . . The average living human possesses a dexterity level 90 percent greater than the strongest ghoul."[13] Beginning with *28 Days Later*, however, the idea of "fast zombies" has made serious inroads into the canon. In Zack Snyder's 2004 remake of *Dawn of the Dead* as well as Charlie Brooker's miniseries *Dead Set* (2008), zombies sprinted at high speeds. In *Zombieland*, the undead spread because they were faster than the aerobically challenged Americans. Frozen Nazi zombies were able to traverse difficult, snowy terrain at high speed in Tommy Wirkola's *Dead Snow* (2009). In Kirkman's *The Walking Dead*, the walkers can turn into runners when they pursue the living. This need for speed prompted Romero to rebut the idea of fast zombies in *Diary of the Dead* (2008). His protagonist explained early on that "dead things don't move fast. . . . If you run that fast, your ankles are gonna snap off."

This debate has clearly animated the zombie studies community—but, again, it is largely irrelevant to questions about international relations. The reason is that, regardless of whether flesh-devouring ghouls move slowly or quickly, the plague of the undead is extremely likely to cross borders. If zombies were able to move and infect humans at high speeds, it would be virtually impossible to contain their spread to a single country or region.[14] However, even if zombies are slow, they are unlikely to stay confined to a single country. A slow-moving zombie outbreak would translate into an equally slow-moving policy response—and, as we shall see in the chapter "Bureaucratic Politics: The 'Pulling and Hauling' of Zombies," the initial responses are likely to be riddled with error.

Furthermore, if the zombie canon is any guide, slow zombies are strongly and positively correlated with a slower incubation period.[15] The infected in *28 Days Later* are fast zombies; when they are exposed to the rage virus, they "turn" in less than thirty seconds. The zombies in Romero's movies or Brooks's *World War Z* are slow moving; if they are bitten, it takes them hours or days to become part of the living dead.* The effect of zombiism corresponds with the speed of transmission. Fast-acting viruses lead to fast zombies, and slow-acting viruses lead to "old school" zombies.

If it takes a longer time for human beings to die and turn into flesh-eating ghouls, then it is also possible for them to travel a farther distance from the original point of infection while still human. With a modern transport infrastructure, an infected individual can get from one major population center to another within twenty-four hours. Even a single outbreak of corpse reanimation can go global. In addition, although the zombie plague is only spread through biting or other fluidic transfers, the infection rate is 100 percent.

---

*Marc Forster's 2013 film adaptation of *World War Z* changed the zombie pathogen from slow to very, very fast. Individuals became zombies in as little as eleven seconds and then moved as fast as the computer-generated imagery programming would allow. And the less said about this the better.

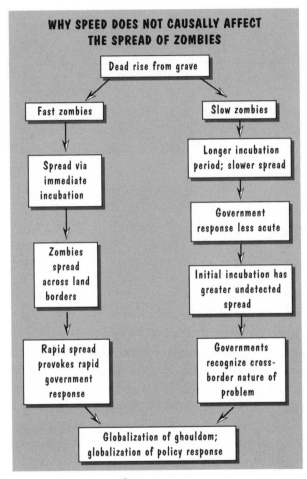

Figure 5. Why speed does not causally affect
the spread of zombies.

TABLE 1
A 2×2 Table, as Required in all Political Science Research

	Fast Zombies	*Slow Zombies*
Supernatural Origins	Cross-border security problem	Cross-border security problem
Scientific Origins	Cross-border Security problem	Cross-border Security problem

Even powerful disease vectors like smallpox or influenza have infection rates that are considerably lower.[16] Because the zombie contagion is so powerful, its cross-border spread is a near certainty.

It should be stressed that the fast-versus-slow debate is of significant importance for other policy dimensions. The military tactics, evacuation logistics, refugee policies, and homeland security measures needed to cope with a fast zombie outbreak would look dramatically different from a slow one. Indeed, US Strategic Command noted in their counterzombie plan that, "there is no 'one size fits all' for counter-zombie operations."[17] We are concerned with global responses in this book, however. As figure 5 demonstrates, both the fast and slow zombie possibilities lead to the same outcome—the globalization of ghouldom. Because either variety of zombie leads to an international relations problem, we can dismiss the *causal* importance of speed as a determining factor in global policy responses. Indeed, as the two-by-two diagram in table 1 demonstrates, neither the origins nor the speed of zombies is of much causal significance.

The starting point of our analysis is that the living dead are a transnational phenomenon. Either corpses reanimate across the globe or they spread outward from a single source. Either way they are a threat that all countries must consider in crafting their foreign and national security policies.

And so we arrive at our central question: What would different theories of international relations predict would happen if the zombies started to roam the earth?

THE *REALPOLITIK* OF THE LIVING DEAD

There are many varieties of realism,[1] but all realists start with a common assumption—that anarchy is the overarching constraint of world politics. Anarchy does not mean chaos or disorder but instead the absence of a centralized, legitimate authority. No matter what ardent cosmopolitans or conspiracy theorists believe, there is no world government. With no monopoly on the use of force in world politics, every actor must adopt "self-help" measures to ensure continued existence. For realists, the primary actors are those that can guarantee their own survival—namely, states. Because force is the ne plus ultra of power, the actors that count are those with the greatest ability to use force—states with sizable armed forces.

Most realists argue that the combination of anarchy and the need for self-help creates recurrent and persistent patterns in international affairs. In a world of anarchy, the only currency that matters is power—the material capability to ward off pressure or coercion while being able to influence others. If one state amasses more and more power, other states will have an incentive to balance against that state so as to prevent it from dominating everyone.[2] The anarchic global structure makes it impossible for governments to fully trust each other, forcing all states to be guided solely by their own national interests.

Since all states can only count on their own resources and capabilities, realists are very skeptical about the ability of international institutions to regulate world politics. States will consider the distribution of gains when thinking about cooperating with another actor. The question for realists like Kenneth Waltz is not "will both of us gain?" but "who will gain more?"[3] Cooperation in the form of balancing coalitions will always be transient and unstable. Just as zombies will always crave human flesh, realpolitik states will always crave a more favorable distribution of capabilities. When relative gains concerns are paramount, cooperation is always ephemeral.[4]

Because anarchy is such a powerful constraint on state actions, realists are not particularly interested in the domestic politics of other countries. Whether a country has a democratic, autocratic, or revolutionary form of government has only a marginal effect on that country's foreign policy trajectory. The structure of anarchy is so powerful that it eventually forces all states into roughly similar policy preferences—maximizing security. This does not necessarily translate into power maximization. States that become too powerful risk triggering what is called a security dilemma—that is, acquiring so much power that other countries choose form a balancing coalition against the rising power.[5] Even realist scholars who believe in power maximization allow that the "stopping power of water" will likely deter any state from global overreach.[6] Realists acknowledge that, on occasion, states deviate from these predictions because of domestic interests.[7] When this happens, however, the competitive rigors of the system will force these actors to either change their behavior—or they will wither away faster than a rotting corpse.[8]

Realists focus like a laser beam on the international distribution of power. The waxing and waning of states corresponds to their influence over outcomes in world politics. Most realists posit that balance-of-power politics acts as a natural regulating mechanism. Power transition theorists, however, care about the relationship between the most powerful state—the hegemon—and potential challengers to its primacy in world politics. If a hegemon is supplanted by a rising power, the likelihood of a great power war spikes.[9] When this situation has occurred in the past—from Sparta and Athens in ancient Greece to Great Britain and Germany prior to World War I—the world becomes fraught with uncertainty. In the past, the prospect of such a power transition has often triggered great power wars. If the rising power signals that it has revisionist aims—in other words, it wants to rewrite the existing rules of world order—then such a conflict will be inexorable.

As this summary might suggest, realism has a rather dystopic and jaundiced view of the world. In other words, realism is perfectly comfortable in the zombie universe—particularly the world of George Romero's films. In the original _Night of the Living Dead_ (1968), seven people are trapped in a farmhouse surrounded by flesh-eating ghouls. Despite the common external threat posed by zombies, the individuals inside the house are barely able to cooperate. Ties of kinship mean little. Two separate sovereign entities (the basement and the first floor) are quickly created and ruled by separate individuals (Harry and Ben).* Resources —food, access to information, firearms—are the object of fierce distributional conflict. Temporary accords designed to create a public good—escape and rescue—quickly break down when there are shifts in the distribution of power.

A similar dynamic plays itself out in Romero's _Dawn of the Dead_ (1978). This time a band of survivors fortifies itself inside a shopping mall. Despite possessing an abundance of resources, the main characters do their utmost to prevent another cluster of

*Indeed, Ben tells Harry, "If you stay up here, you take orders from _me_!"

humans from entering the mall.* When a biker gang breaches their defenses, they respond by opening the docking bays to let in more zombies—to occupy the attention of the bikers. Cooperation breaks down in Romero's *Day of the Dead* (1985) as well—indeed, the character of Sarah complains early on in that film that "we're all pulling in different directions."

The realist imprint on the zombie canon is hardly limited to Romero. Robert Kirkman's *The Walking Dead* (2010–) also stresses that the threats that emanate from anarchy are greater than the threats posed by the living dead. In the first season, Glenn is taken captive by a rival group of human survivors in Atlanta. Rick negotiates his release with the leader of the other group, who—paraphrasing Thucydides—explains that even in a postzombie world "it's the same as it ever was. The weak get taken." Most interactions with other human groups lead inexorably to violent conflict. Once Rick's group manages to establish sovereignty over a prison complex, it triggers a security dilemma with the neighboring territory of Woodbury. Relations between Rick's group and The Governor's group quickly become zero-sum. As enduring rivals, The Governor and Rick attack each other again and again and again in a seem-

---

*As the biker gang rampages the mall, Stephen mutters, "It's ours. We took it. It's ours." He then starts shooting the bikers.

ingly endless cycle of conflict. The failure of humans to cooperate in the presence of reanimated corpses is a common theme that permeates the zombie canon—just as the futility of international cooperation recurs throughout the realist interpretation of history.

How would the introduction of flesh-eating ghouls affect world politics? The realist answer is simple, if surprising: international relations would be largely unaffected. This paradigm would be unimpressed with the claim that a new existential threat to the human condition leads to any radical change in human behavior. Indeed, realists would share the perspective of Major West in Danny Boyle's *28 Days Later* (2002) about the effect of the zombie apocalypse: "This is what I've seen in the four weeks since infection: people killing people. Which is much what I saw in the four weeks before infection, and the four weeks before that, and before that, as far back as I care to remember—people killing people. Which, to my mind, puts us in a state of normality right now."

To realists, a plague of the undead would merely echo older plagues and disasters. Disease has affected world politics from the Black Death of the fourteenth century to the 1918–19 influenza pandemic. In the past, most of these plagues simply reified existing power relationships. Because more dynamic and powerful societies developed stronger immunities to plague, they gained a greater share of relative power during pandemics.[10] Similarly, modern research shows that wealthier and more powerful societies can weather natural disasters better than weaker, poorer states.[11] Realists would see no reason to expect an epidemic of zombies to be any different in its effects. US Strategic Command concurs, concluding that, "countries with more advanced, prepared and robust health care and agricultural systems . . . will be better able to mitigate many of the zombie phenomena effects."[12] To paraphrase Thucydides, the realpolitik of zombies is that the strong will do what they can, and the weak must suffer devouring by reanimated, ravenous corpses.

To be sure, even realists would acknowledge *some* shifts in the global distribution of power from the reanimation of the dead. Some governments will be better placed to repulse the zombies than others. Those with greater security and communications infrastructures should be able to put down any internal zombie insurrections and reestablish domestic order or block cross-border zombie incursions. States with low population densities would have more time to adapt to the presence of the undead. Geographic isolation would be no guarantee of zombie prevention. As Romero demonstrated in *Land of the Dead* (2005) and Max Brooks showed in his novel *World War Z* (2006), the stopping power of water for the undead is limited because they have no need to breathe.* Nev-

---

*One exception might be the implication in Charlie Brooker's miniseries *Dead Set* (2008) that fast zombies are helpless when confronted with water—even if it is just a kiddie pool.

ertheless, geography still matters. Some geographic features alter the offense-defense balance vis-à-vis an external attack—in other words, defense is easier than offense on certain kinds of terrain, such as coastlines or mountain ranges.[13] Realists would expect countries with mountainous borders to be more likely to thwart hordes of foreign flesh-eating ghouls. Some states would undoubtedly be completely overrun by the living dead.

Would the *character* of world politics change, however? Not necessarily. The best tactics and strategies for defeating zombies would spread quickly throughout the international system, regardless of the ethical or moral implications of such plans. In *World War Z*, for example, the national security strategy that diffuses throughout the globe has its origins in an apartheid South African government's doomsday scenario of an all-out uprising by the black population.[14] This strategy calls for the intentional sacrifice of some population centers. Given the exigencies of the situation, however, it is quickly adopted worldwide.

Realists also predict balance-of-power politics. Wouldn't the specter of the undead create a balancing coalition against all ghouls? This possibility cannot be ruled out, particularly for power transition theorists. If zombies emerged from central Eurasia, for example, their capacity to spread quickly could trigger a natural balancing coalition designed to prevent zombie hordes from spreading across the entire

Eurasian landmass. If ghouls overran a significant cluster of states and created a sufficient number of fresh ghouls, a power transition dynamic could present itself. Posthuman actors would be seen as the rapidly rising power—and no one would deny that their preference for human flesh would represent radically revisionist war aims. A containment strategy would no doubt be proposed as a means of limiting the territorial expansion of the undead.[15]

Most realists would be very skeptical about the robustness of a universal antizombie alliance, however. First, *buck-passing* would be an equally likely outcome.[16] In a buck-passing situation, states would refrain from taking an active stance against the zombie hordes in the hopes that other countries would do the dirty work of balancing in their stead. So even if a powerful state tried to amass an antizombie coalition, other governments might commit to such an alliance in name only.

Second, small supporter states would fear that powerful countries would use a global quest against zombies as a subterfuge to augment their own capabilities and interests. Past history offers some support for this prediction. The Soviet Union installed puppet governments in its military theater of operations at the end of World War II to develop a buffer zone between itself and the Western alliance. Even during the peak period of the Cold War, NATO members repeatedly clashed over the scope and nature of the strategic embargo placed on the communist bloc, because some members of the Western alliance benefited disproportionately from trade with the Soviet Union.[17] A similar dynamic played itself out during the American-led "global war on terror" in the early part of this century. The United States tried to coordinate global efforts against all nonstate actors that employed this tactic. Other countries responded by adding groups that were considered national threats but did not quite fit the definition of terrorist.[18]

Realists would predict a similar dynamic at work in any kind of antizombie crusade, except on an even grander scope. In the past, natural disasters have exacerbated preexisting conflicts among humans.[19] States could therefore exploit the threat from the living dead to acquire new territory, squelch irredentist movements, settle old scores, or subdue enduring rivals. The People's Republic of China could use the zombie threat to justify an occupation of Taiwan. Russia could use the same excuse to justify intervention into its near abroad; in the novel *World War Z*, the conflict allows Moscow to reabsorb Belarus. India and Pakistan would likely accuse each other of failing to control the zombie problem in Kashmir.* The United States would not be immune from the temptation to exploit the zombie threat as a strategic opportunity. How

---

*In *World War Z*, Pakistan's failure to control its zombie infestation leads to a militarized dispute with Iran.

large would the army of the Cuban undead need to be to justify the deployment of the Eighty-Second Airborne Division? In the end, realists—particularly American realists—would no doubt evoke the cautionary words of former president John Quincy Adams and warn against going abroad "in search of monsters to destroy."

Some realists would go further, arguing that, in the end, human-zombie alliances of convenience would be just as likely to emerge as human-human alliances. As previously noted, some zombies in the canon start out possessing strategic intelligence, making them more than capable of recognizing the virtues of tactical agreements with some humans. Many zombie studies scholars might object to this point, arguing that flesh-eating ghouls can neither talk nor develop strategic thought. Even if they did not, though, realists would point to Romero's zombies for empirical support. As early as *Night of the Living Dead*, Romero's ghouls demonstrated the capacity for using tools.* In each of his subsequent films, the undead grew more cognitively complex. The zombie characters of Bub in *Day of the Dead* and Big Daddy in *Land of the Dead* were painted with a more sympathetic brush than most of the human characters. Both Bub and Big Daddy learned how to use firearms. Bub was able to speak,

*The very first zombie we see in *Night of the Living Dead* uses a rock to break into Barbara's car.

perform simple tasks, and exercise impulse control —that is, to refrain from eating a human he liked. Big Daddy and his undead cohort developed a hierarchical authority structure with the ability to engage in tactical and strategic learning. In doing so they overran a well-fortified human redoubt and killed its most powerful leader. It would take only the mildest of cognitive leaps to envision a zombie-articulated defense of these actions at the United Nations.

By the end of *Land of the Dead* the lead zombie character and the lead human character acknowledge a tacit bargain to leave each other alone. This is perfectly consistent with the realist paradigm. For zombies to survive and thrive, they must avoid losing their brains; and, like humans, they also must adapt to the rigors of anarchy in world politics. While some emerging zombie governments might pursue radical antihuman policies at first, the anarchical system would eventually discipline a moderation of views.[20]

In a world of sophisticated zombies, alliances between human states and zombie states are possible. Indeed, any government that tried to develop a grand coalition targeting the undead would immediately trigger the security dilemma. Realpolitik states could exploit any move toward an idealistic global war on zombies by creating temporary alliances of convenience with emerging ghoul governments. A more passive strategy would be to encourage what John

Zombies could defend their actions at the United Nations.

Mearsheimer labels "bait and bleed" and "bloodletting" strategies.[21] In these instances, realist states would try to foment conflict between antizombie states and the ghouls themselves, profiting at the relative losses incurred by both sides. In Kirkman's *The Walking Dead*, The Governor perfects a similar strategy, killing people so that they will reanimate into zombies later, thereby wreaking havoc on adversaries.

Realists would advocate noninterference in how zombie states treated their own living and undead populations.* In the end, realists would conclude that there would be little intrinsic difference between human states and zombie states. Human beings have an innate lust for power in the realist paradigm; zombies have an innate lust for human flesh. Both are scarce resources. Regardless of individual traits, domestic institutions, or variations in the desire for living flesh, human and zombie actors alike are subject to the same powerful constraint of anarchy. Both sets of actors would engage in strategic opportunism to advance their interests in anarchy. The fundamental character of world politics would therefore remain unchanged. In the end, realists would caution human governments against expending significant amounts of blood and treasure to engage in far-flung antizombie adventures—particularly blood.

*Some realists would no doubt warn against the power of a "human lobby" to blind governments from their national interests.

REGULATING THE UNDEAD IN A LIBERAL WORLD ORDER

Like the realist paradigm, there are many varieties of liberalism.[1] All liberals nevertheless share a common belief: cooperation is still possible in a world of anarchy. Liberals look at world politics as a non-zero-sum game. Mutual cooperation on issues ranging from international trade to nuclear nonproliferation to disease prevention can yield global public goods on a massive scale. These gains are not always distributed evenly, but they do make all actors better off than they would be in the absence of policy coordination. Major actors in world politics therefore have an incentive to realize the benefits that come from long-term mutual cooperation and avoid the costs that come with mutual defection.

Liberals do not believe that cooperative outcomes always happen in world politics. In some cases, preferences might be so divergent that no bargain can be struck among the actors. Even if a non-zero-sum bargain is possible, the incentive to realize these gains does not guarantee that collaboration takes place. The benefits generated by cooperation are often nonexcludable—in other words, anyone will benefit from broad-based cooperation even if they themselves do not cooperate. For example, if a plucky band of survivors were to devise a way to eliminate the plague of the undead, all humans would benefit regardless of whether they helped or not. This creates a *free-rider problem*, as the payoff structure in table 2 demonstrates. The conundrum for liberals is that while an outcome of mutual cooperation is better than one of mutual defection, all are best off in a situation in which they can unilaterally defect. Since every actor has these same incentives, the outcome can be a "tragedy of the commons"—everyone defecting, even though everyone is better off cooperating.[2]

This situation is not hopeless, however. The liberal paradigm offers multiple strategies to overcome the tragedy of the commons.[3] Conditions that lengthen the shadow of the future increase the likelihood of cooperation. The longer one's time horizon, the greater the rewards from mutual cooperation are in comparison to the fleeting benefits from free riding. If an actor expects to be around for a while, then response strategies that punish noncooperation but play well with "nice" actors—such as tit for tat—can sustain multilateral cooperation over the long run.

TABLE 2
Tragedy of the Commons Game

		Player B	
		Cooperate	Defect
Player A	Cooperate	(3,3)	(0,5)
	Defect	(5,0)	(1,1)

Other gambits can increase the rewards from cooperation and reduce the benefits from defection. Economic interdependence reduces the incentive to defect by magnifying the gap in gains between a world of collective action and a world of mutual distrust.[4] Governments will be less likely to cheat in the short term if they know it means they will lose the benefits from trade in the long term. Multilateral institutions that monitor and disseminate information can ensure that cheating will be detected and punished.[5] Institutions reassure all participating actors that they are on the same page in terms of the rules of the game—and they clarify how and when those rules will be broken.

Finally, democracies are more likely to cooperate with each other. Liberals posit that democracies are more likely to have similar preferences, making cooperation easier. More significantly, domestic laws and institutions provide democracies with the means to credibly commit to international agreements.[6]

Liberals allow that the Hobbesian war of all against all predicted by realism could happen, but only under very extreme conditions.[7] A world of economic interdependence, democratic governments, and international institutions should foster extensive amounts of multilateral cooperation.

At first glance, the liberal paradigm appears to be a bad fit for a zombie genre that specializes in apocalypses. Indeed, the tragedy of liberalism in a universe with zombies is that some of its central tenets would accelerate the spread of flesh-eating ghouls. Liberals advocate an open global economy in order to foster complex interdependence and lock in incentives for governments to cooperate. Just as open borders foster greater migration of peoples and pandemics, they would also facilitate the cross-border spread of both the undead and infected human carriers.[8] In sharp contrast to realism, liberal policy prescriptions would appear to exacerbate the first stages of the zombie menace. It is little wonder, therefore, that so many critical theorists equate the unchecked spread of zombies with the unchecked spread of capitalism itself.[9]

Similarly, liberals acknowledge that sustainable cooperation with zombies would be next to impossible. One would be hard-pressed to devise sanctions that would compel zombies into cooperating. The divergence of preferences is also too great. The refrain in Jonathan Coulton's song "Re: Your Brains," written from a zombie's point of view, best encapsulates the implacable nature of the zombie bargaining position:

All we want to do is eat your brains
We're not unreasonable; I mean, no one's gonna eat
    your eyes
All we want to do is eat your brains
We're at an impasse here; maybe we should
    compromise:
If you open up the doors
We'll all come inside and eat your brains

If this represents the zombie bargaining position, then the liberal assumption of a non-zero-sum bargain does not hold. As table 3 shows, in the Tragedy of the Zombies game, the dominant strategy for zombies is to eat humans. Tit-for-tat strategies do not work. Neither cooperation nor coordination is possible with the living dead.

A deeper cut, however, reveals that the liberal paradigm can offer significant analytical bite. Romantic zombie comedies—rom-zom-coms, for short—contain both implicit and explicit elements of liberalism. Ruben Fleischer's *Zombieland* (2009) is about the articulation and adherence to well-defined rules for surviving in a zombie-infested landscape. Its central message—beyond the need for cardio workouts—is the need for disparate individuals to credibly commit to each other. The characters in Edgar Wright's

TABLE 3
Tragedy of the Zombies Game

		Humans	
		Don't kill zombies	Kill zombies
Zombies	Don't eat humans	(1,4)	(0,5)
	Eat humans	(5,0)	(4,1)

Shaun of the Dead (2004) cooperate with each other far more than in any of George Romero's films. Indeed, just before the climax, the characters find themselves trapped inside a structure surrounded by the living dead. The scenario is identical to Romero's *Night of the Living Dead* (1968), except that these characters are in a pub rather than a farmhouse. Contra Romero, however, in this film Shaun rallies his friends and relations with a stirring paean to liberalism: "As Bertrand Russell once said, 'the only thing that will redeem mankind is cooperation.' I think we can all appreciate the relevance of that now."

The liberal paradigm offers some intriguing predictions and explanations for how a global zombie outbreak could affect world politics. Perhaps the most important liberal insight is a possible answer to one of the biggest mysteries in zombie studies—the failure of ghouls to ever attack each other. In Romero's *Dawn of the Dead* (1978), a scientist observes that "there are no divisions" among the undead. Even those suffering from the "rage virus" in Danny

Boyle's *28 Days Later* (2002) focus their rage only on other humans—not their fellow infected. We assume that zombies have no wish to eat each other, but it is surprising that they do not turn on each other when trying to divvy up a human carcass—especially as human flesh grows scarce. From Romero's *Night of the Living Dead* (1968) onward, however, zombies have either tolerated each other's company or actively cooperated to defeat humans.

Why? The liberal paradigm provides a simple, rational answer: the living dead have the longest possible shadow of the future. John Maynard Keynes famously commented that "in the long run, we are all dead." In the long run, the undead still have to interact with each other—and therefore they have the strongest of incentives to cooperate.[10] If zombies hang together, then humans face the danger of hanging separately.

Despite the daunting degree of zombie solidarity, liberals would predict that the incentive for multilateral cooperation among humans would be powerful as well. The proliferation of the differently animated represents a classic *negative externality* problem of economic globalization. Countries that profit from trading with each other would nevertheless reward a third party—flesh-eating ghouls—by unwittingly facilitating their spread. States would therefore view zombies the same way they viewed other public bads that emerged from the open global economy, such as money laundering or food-borne diseases. Powerful governments would create and reinforce international institutions designed to control their spread. The US Centers for Disease Control and Prevention publicly pledged to provide technical assistance to "international partners" should the dead start to rise from the grave.[11] Indeed, the zombie menace would touch so many different spheres of life that liberals would predict a "regime complex" to emerge.[12] A welter of international governmental organizations—including the United Nations Security Council, the World Health Organization, and the International Organization for Migration—would promulgate a series of policies and protocols designed to combat existing zombie hordes and prevent further outbreaks.* A coordinating body, perhaps even a World Zombie Organization (WZO), would need to be formed in order to handle all of the overlapping health, trade, and security issues. In the end, some organization would announce a "comprehensive and integrated dezombiefication strategy," with sufficient buy-in from stakeholders across global civil society, as their plan of action.**

*Given that zombies would be covered under genetically modified organisms, the European Union would immediately invoke the Cartagena Protocol on Biosafety as the key regulatory mechanism for the cross-border movement of reanimated dead tissue.

**This liberal prediction hinges crucially on whether the initial policy responses could mitigate the spread of ghouls. If decision maker concluded that no action could halt the spread of the undead, then the shadow of the future would disappear; liberals would predict actors to pursue endgame strategies of noncooperation. Hiding and hoarding would be the appropriate responses at this juncture.

The liberal expectation would be that a counter-zombie regime complex could make significant inroads into the zombie problem. The public benefits of wiping the undead from the face of the earth are quite significant, boosting the likelihood of significant policy coordination.[13] The undead would fall into the category of systemic threats—such as terrorism and global pandemics—where states have engaged in meaningful cross-border cooperation. This prediction is also consistent with key portions of the zombie literature. In Max Brooks's novel *World War Z* (2006), the decision to go on the offensive comes after a United Nations meeting.[14] Consistent with liberal internationalism, the United States provided the necessary leadership and a strong sense of social purpose in order to rally support.[15]

How effective would these global governance structures be in combating the undead? The question of regime effectiveness has haunted international relations scholarship for decades.[16] To be sure, liberal security regimes such as NATO or the Chemical Weapons Convention have a credible track record of success.[17] The ability of both security and health regimes to monitor and spread information quickly in the era of instant messaging would facilitate rapid reactions to the zombie problem at an early stage. Globalization has certainly fostered the technical and regulatory coordination necessary for enhancing biosecurity.[18] At a minimum, one would expect a significant rollback and stringent regulation of the living dead, roughly consistent with the start of Andrew Currie's *Fido* (2006) or the outcome in Mira Grant's *Feed* (2010).[19]

Although the macrosituation might appear stable, it would also be imperfect. At present, the regime for cross-border movement of the dead already has significant loopholes.[20] Even if the vagaries of current international law are fixed, zombies represent a tough test for global governance structures. They are the most difficult kind of governance problem—a prohibition regime.[21] Unless every single ghoul is hunted down and destroyed beyond recognition, a recurrent spread of the undead remains a possibility. The international regimes designed to eliminate disease demonstrate the difficulties inherent in this task. The scourge of smallpox has been erased, but few other diseases have been completely and totally eradicated.[22] The persistence of AIDS, polio, malaria, tuberculosis, and the myriad strains of influenza demonstrate the challenges that would face an international counterzombie regime.

The liberal paradigm would predict two significant loopholes that could form within the confines of a global counterzombie regime. First, some countries might fail to provide timely information about zombie outbreaks until the problem had escalated beyond local control. Authoritarian countries are often reluctant to admit health crises because of the threat such an admission could have on state control over society. In Alejandro Brugués's *Juan of the Dead* (2011), for example, the Cuban government initially labels the living dead as American-supported dissidents. Furthermore, as will be discussed in the chapter "Domestic Politics: Are All Zombie Politics Local?" nondemocratic regimes are less likely to invest in the public goods necessary to prevent or contain disasters.[23] This is one reason why the loss of life from disasters is greater in authoritarian countries.[24] Local officials could delay reporting a zombie outbreak up the chain of command for fear of being the bearer of bad news. Developing countries might lack the infrastructure to detect the reemergence of the living dead. They would certainly fear the economic impact of any policy response by large market jurisdiction to an announced outbreak of flesh-eating ghouls.* China's initial refusal to notify the rest of the world of its cases of severe acute respiratory syndrome (SARS) in a timely, transparent, and verifiable manner in 2002–3 is an exemplary case of this kind of policy conundrum.[25] China behaves in a similar manner in *World War Z*—going so far as to trigger a crisis with Taiwan to disguise the extent of China's own zombie problem.[26]

---

*This problem is not limited to developing countries. If flesh-eating ghouls were detected, two immediate and obvious predictions would follow: the European Union would impose a complete ban on British beef, and Japan and South Korea would impose a similar ban on US beef.

Protests against counterzombie
policies would be unsurprising.

Second, it would not be surprising if nongovern-
mental organizations (NGOs) devoted to the defense
of the living dead acted as an impediment to their
eradication. The ability of NGOs to alter global governance structures is a matter of some debate within
international relations scholarship.[27] At a minimum,

however, global civil society can raise the transaction costs of implementing the rules of global governance. At least one nonprofit organization in favor of zombie equality already exists—Great Britain's Citizens for Undead Rights and Equality.[28] The formation of more powerful activist groups—Zombie Rights Watch, Zombies without Borders, ZombAid, People for the Ethical Treatment of Zombies, or Occupy Human Streets—would undoubtedly make it difficult for a WZO to achieve perfect eradication. The likelihood of a ZombieLeaks entity publishing sensitive and classified information about the counterzombie regime seems strong.

While these pitfalls could prove problematic, they should not be overstated. China has moved down the learning curve as a result of the SARS episode; authorities in Beijing were much more transparent during the 2009 H1N1 swine flu epidemic, for example.[29] As countries have adapted to the problem of pandemics, fewer of them would be expected to conceal a growing problem with the undead. Even if multilateral solutions proved to be inadequate, liberals would envision the emergence of "minilateral" or regional organizations to act as a backstop. The United States would likely respond to any failure of a WZO by creating a North American Counterzombie Agreement to handle the problem regionally. Similarly, one would expect the European Commission to issue the mother of all directives to cope with the issue.* The Association of Southeast Asian Nations, Mercosur, the Arab League, and the African Union would not be far behind. The bulk of global civil society would also be unlikely to raise too much of an objection to the eradication of the undead. Zombie rights would likely be one of those issues that more powerful NGOs would resist pushing on their advocacy agenda for fear of triggering donor fatigue or political backlash.[30]

The liberal paradigm would predict an outcome that would be imperfect and vulnerable to political criticism over time—much like the European Union in its current form. That said, the system would also be expected to function well enough to ward off the specter of a total zombie apocalypse. Zombie flare-ups would no doubt take place. Quasi-permanent humanitarian counterzombie missions, under United Nations auspices, would likely be necessary in failed states. Liberals would acknowledge the permanent eradication of flesh-eating ghouls as unlikely. The reduction of the zombie problem to one of many manageable threats, however, would be a foreseeable outcome. To use the lexicon of liberals, most governments would kill most zombies most of the time.

---

*It is beyond the scope of this text to discuss how zombie comitology within the European Union would be handled. There is little doubt, however, that it would be painful.

THE SOCIAL CONSTRUCTION
OF ZOMBIES

Constructivism is the most recent international relations paradigm to achieve widespread scholarly recognition. Just as with the realist and liberal paradigms, there exists a plethora of constructivist approaches.[1] Constructivist approaches do share a set of core assumptions about world politics, however. These assumptions and causal mechanisms revolve around two central tenets: the social construction of reality, and the importance of identity in explaining and interpreting behavior on the world stage.

For constructivists, material factors such as economic wealth and military power are important—but even more important are how social structures filter and interpret the meaning of those material capabilities. For example, zombies are hardly the only actors in the social world to crave human flesh. Cannibals, sharks, and really hungry bears will also target *Homo sapiens* if there is sufficient opportunity and willingness. Nevertheless, zombies are perceived to be a much greater threat to humankind. Why? There are material factors to consider—to our knowledge, bears can't turn human beings into more bears by biting them. Constructivists would argue that this is an incomplete explanation, however. Zombies threaten the powerful human norm of not devouring each other for sustenance or pleasure—and therefore arouse greater security concerns as a result.

Constructivists argue that transnational norms are a powerful constraint on action in world politics. Nuclear weapons, for example, are the most powerful destructive force in human history—but they have not been used in combat since 1945. Social constructivists argue that, over time, a taboo has developed regarding their use.[2] Within societies, actors will usually refrain from violating powerful social norms because they do not want to be ostracized by their peers. Constructivist scholars argue that this effect also exists in global society; by and large, governments want to avoid being ostracized by other actors in the international community.[3]

Just as important to the constructivist paradigm is the role that identity plays in defining actors and their preferences. Identities are developed or constituted through mutual recognition—authoritative actors are considered legitimate in the international community not only because of self-recognition but because others recognize them as legitimate. Actors—including but not limited to states—define themselves in part by distinguishing themselves from the "other."[4]

This provides all actors a greater sense of ontological security that guides their actions and beliefs in world affairs.[5] Because zombies used to be human, reanimated, ravenous flesh-eating corpses could make humans more uncertain about their identity—and how it differs from the viably challenged.

Significant elements of the zombie canon have a constructivist bent. As cultural critics have observed, the horror in zombie films comes not from a single ghoul but from an ever-expanding community of them.[6] It other words, the terror increases when a large swath of individuals are socialized into the ways of the undead. Similarly, zombie films persistently raise questions about the identity distinctions between ghouls and humans. These questions provoke considerable anxiety—and occasional nightmares—from human protagonists. One recent cultural analysis of the zombie genre observes, "What is remarkable about so many zombie movies is that the survivors of the plague/accident/alien invasion that caused the infection do so little to distinguish themselves from zombies; it's very much a case of *as you are, so too am I*."[7] In George Romero's films, characters cannot escape commenting on the similarities between the living and the undead. The actions of the zombies and the zombie-hunting posse in *Night of the Living Dead* (1968) are barely distinguishable from each other. In both *Dawn of the Dead* (1978) and *Day of the Dead*

(1985) a human character, discussing the zombies, simply declares, "They're us." The most iconic line in Robert Kirkman's *Walking Dead* comic book (2005) comes when Rick Grimes shouts in anger and despair to the rest of his group, "We *are* the walking dead!"

One could argue that social constructivism is better prepared than other paradigms to deal with a paranormal phenomenon like the dead rising from the grave. As previously noted, constructivists have engaged with other paranormal actors, such as UFOs. The applicability of these preexisting theoretical arguments to zombies is open to question, however. For example, Alexander Wendt and Raymond Duvall's constructivist explanation of official denials of extraterrestrial aliens is premised on the notion that these aliens possess technology superior to that of humans.[8] The technological superiority of aliens undercuts the anthropocentric nature of human worldviews. UFOs therefore go unacknowledged because any official recognition would endanger the sovereignty of *Homo sapiens* on Planet Earth. While zombies possess a tactical comparative advantage over humans in already being dead, their technological capabilities are far lower. Indeed, Wendt and Duvall's arguments cannot be extended to vampires, ghosts, Elvis Presley, or the Loch Ness monster—much less zombies. Unfortunately, attempting to advance this UFO-specific variant of constructivism further would represent a theoretical dead end.

The constructivist paradigm nevertheless offers some useful predictions and policy recommendations. If confronted with the exogenous shock of the undead, constructivists would undoubtedly argue that zombies are what humans make of them.[9] That is to say, there are a number of possible emergent orders in response to zombies. One possible norm could be the Hobbesian "kill or be killed" scenario in which human beings turn on each other as well as the living dead. Some research,[10] as well as most of the zombie canon, concludes that the natural response to the rise of the living dead would be sheer panic, leading to genuine anarchy.

Most constructivists would instead posit that a Kantian "pluralistic counter-zombie security community" in which governments share sovereignty and resources to combat the undead menace is more likely.[11] Empirical work on how individuals respond to manufactured and natural disasters suggests that this is the more likely outcome than that predicted in George Romero's oeuvre.[12] Rebecca Solnit observes that "in the wake of an earthquake, a bombing, or a major storm, most people are altruistic, urgently engaged in caring for themselves and those around them, strangers and neighbors as well as friends and loved ones. The image of the selfish, panicky, or regressively savage human being in times of disaster has little truth to it."[13] Anthropological research further suggests that only with extreme resource scarcity will communities of people turn on each other.[14]

This could hold with even greater force if flesh-eating ghouls are the source of the disaster. The existence of zombies might foster some initial onto-logical insecurity, but over time the implacable nature of the zombie threat should create a stronger feel-ing of collective identity among humans—because they have no intrinsic compulsion to consume the entrails of the living.[15] This shared sense of identity should, in turn, foster a greater sense of ontological security. Indeed, for some constructivists, the existen-tial peril posed by zombies could be the exogenous shock needed to break down nationalist divides and advance the creation of a world state.[16]

To nudge key actors toward the creation of a plu-ralistic security community in response to zombies, constructivists would offer two controversial but concrete policy recommendations. The first preemp-tive move would be to destroy every copy of nearly every zombie film ever made. Intentionally or unin-tentionally, constructivists argue that the consistency of the zombie narrative socially constructs "apoca-lypse myths." As Frank Furedi observes, "The ex-perience of disasters—major and minor—is a social phenomenon which is mediated through the public's cultural imagination."[17] Cultural narratives that sug-gest panic, disaster, and mayhem can have real-world effects.[18] If everyone expects the rise of living dead to trigger panic and dystopia, then those misperceptions could very well reify that outcome. The zombie canon stresses the dog-eat-dog (or person-eat-person) nature of undead apocalypses. Those images could become cemented in both elite and mass public perceptions. At the very least, security institutions should subsidize countervailing narratives about resilience in the face of flesh-eating ghouls—something that, not coincidentally, occurs in Max Brooks's novel *World War Z* (2006).

The second policy suggestion would be to socialize zombies into human culture. Jen Webb and Sam Byrnard observe that "zombies aren't social isolates—they seem to prefer to live in groups, within built social environments."[19] There are examples in the zombie canon of the living dead learning or adopting human norms of behavior. In Romero's *Day of the Dead*, Dr. Logan suggests that zombies are demonstrating the "bare beginnings of social behavior," allowing for the possibility of human society socializing them. This is certainly the aim in their efforts to "train" Bub. Similarly, at the end of Edgar Wright's *Shaun of the Dead* (2004), a montage demonstrates the ways in which English society reintegrates the remaining zombies—as game show contestants, daytime talk show guests, supermarket workers, and video game players. Over the course of Isaac Marion's *Warm Bodies*

(2011), the zombie R slowly eschews zombie tropes and begins to embrace human norms and behaviors. All of these examples would be consistent with the socialization efforts advocated by constructivist scholars. If the undead learn to act as if they are human again, then constructivists would posit that they have abandoned their identity as flesh-eating ghouls.

These policy recommendations are potentially useful, but a thorough constructivist analysis would have to acknowledge a darker possibility. The suggested constructivist policies assume that once zombies walk the earth, humans will be able to socialize them before they proliferate beyond human control. If a critical mass of flesh-eating ghouls were to emerge, however, then the constructivist paradigm offers a very different prediction. Constructivists would predict an emergent "norm cascade" from the proliferation of the living dead.[20] A norm cascade functions like peer pressure: as people witness others adhering to a particular standard of behavior, they are more likely to conform to that standard of behavior as well. As a larger fraction of individuals are converted to the undead persuasion, the remaining humans would feel significant material and social pressure to conform to zombie practices.

The conformity meme appears frequently in the zombie canon. In *World War Z*, Brooks notes the existence of "quislings," humans who act like they are zombies. As one character describes them, "These people were zombies, maybe not physically, but mentally you

The lifestyles of the college
student and zombie are eerily
similar.

could not tell the difference."[21] In *Shaun of the Dead*,
the principal characters practice shuffling and moaning in order to blend in. In Ruben Fleischer's *Zombieland* (2009), Bill Murray puts on zombie makeup in
order to go out for an evening. Even if humans adopt
zombie norms simply to survive, over time these actions will begin to constitute their identity.

Norms acquire general acceptance through a combination of greater numbers and the intrinsic attrac-
tiveness of the practices themselves. While one could
casually dismiss the idea that eating live human flesh

would be attractive, other components of the zombie lifestyle might be alluring to many humans. The living dead do not feel the need to bathe, shave, or change their clothes—nor do they judge each other based on appearance. Zombies do not discriminate based on race, color, creed, ethnicity, or sexual orientation. They always hang out in large packs or herds. They are extremely ecofriendly—zombies walk everywhere and only eat local, organic produce. This description accurately captures many of the lifestyle traits of the typical college student, graduate student, or urban hipster—the change agents of many societies. Zombies might have hidden reserves of soft power, leading humans to want what zombies want.[22] If this cultural vanguard were to embrace zombie normcore as a way of life, or even just as a fashion trend, remaining survivors would eventually internalize all zombie norms. These would include guttural moaning, shuffling, and smelling like death warmed over. In the end, both socialized humans and zombies would crave the flesh of unrepentant humans. At this point, the conceptual category of zombies would not be restricted to reanimated corpses—it would be a social construct as well.

THE SUPERGENDERED
POLITICS OF THE
POSTHUMAN WORLD

Two important aspects about the living dead suggest that mainstream international relations scholars will not truly comprehend the magnitude of the threat. First, because most mainstream scholarship focuses on the state as the principal actor in world politics, researchers working in these traditions might be too slow to appreciate the dreaded risk posed by zombies. Second, one of the most basic yet underdiscussed aspects of zombies is their objectification of human bodies. By definition, the living dead do not view human beings as individuals with thoughts, feelings, and identities, but instead as bodies of tactile, sensual, delicious flesh just waiting to be ravished. Craving human bodies in a way that literally negates the "other" is a preference ordering that is alien to even the most hard-bitten realist.

These two issues, of course, have long been the province of more critical perspectives on international affairs. In particular, one can posit that a feminist approach to international relations is best suited to assess and evaluate the effect of the living dead.[1] According to Mary Deitz, feminist theory has the capacity to utilize a wide array of methodological approaches toward analyzing the world, including but not limited to "critical theory, discourse ethics, political liberalism, analytic philosophy, hermeneutics, structuralism, existentialism, phenomenology, deconstruction, genealogy, poststructuralism, postcolonial theory, psychoanalysis, semiotics, cultural studies, language analysis, pragmatism, neo-Marxism, and post-Marxism."[2] Confronted with this formidable array of analytical tools, the living dead clearly do not stand a chance.

As with the other approaches to international politics, the feminist paradigm covers a heterogeneous family of theories, ranging from liberal feminism to critical feminism to poststructuralism.[3] All feminist approaches share a few key traits, however. The first and most important commonality is that the realities of world politics depend on shared ideas about the attributes of men and women and the role that they can, do, and should play in the world. In short, feminist theorists argue that gender as a set of social constructs about how men and women relate matters to political outcomes we see in the world, even in situations appearing to have nothing to do with gender— such as, say, the specter of the undead.

Second, feminists observe that the realities of world politics—and the international relations theories of world politics—are constructed to marginalize these gendered realities and, by extension, the role of women.[4] This is reflected in mainstream scholarship. The puzzles that animate realists or liberals—the causes of war, the ways states advance their national interests—are framed in such a way as to keep gender on the margins of discourse.[5] To take just one example, the conduct of diplomatic and military statecraft almost always elides the traditional roles of women, which can range from supporting the crucial logistics of diplomatic discourse to providing low-cost migrant labor for the domestic services industry.[6] Even though gendered roles and experiences can at times be central to explaining security outcomes, they are marginalized in both international relations and international relations theory.

The third commonality to all feminist theories is the normative core of the paradigm. "Malestream" scholars believe that their job is to model the world as it is; feminist scholars believe that, in part, their role is to expose the heavily gendered structure of world politics in order to change it for the better.[7] Only by decomposing and deprivileging mainstream paradigms can a feminist approach reveal the myriad ways that modern international relations reifies gender and commits violence against women. Feminist approaches stress that even during periods of peace among nation-states, the world is not really that peaceable toward women. Illuminating these facts can help nudge the system toward a more feminist-friendly equilibrium.[8]

Liberal feminists are aware of the myriad ways in which world politics marginalizes women. They also believe, however, that the emancipation of women from traditionally gendered roles makes it possible for international society to function better. This logic carries over to the liberal feminist analysis of the zombie question; if you add zombies and stir, then what is good for women will also be good for the fight against the living dead. For example, a significant body of research suggests that states that codify gender equality and restrict discrimination are more secure across a variety of dimensions.[9] In other words, governments with more feminist-friendly policies are also more secure from external threats. It logically follows that the threat of the living dead should accelerate those emancipatory policies, thereby benefitting the marginalized even more.

Liberal feminists can point to aspects of the zombie canon that are consistent with this argument. In Zack Snyder's remake of *Dawn of the Dead* (2004), for example, a group of survivors make their way into a mall, only to find themselves under the control of the white, male, heterosexual patriarchy of the mall security guards. This period of governance is portrayed as highly dysfunctional, with repeated conflict and restrictions placed on personal freedoms. Once the survivors take over, however, the resulting governance structure changes for the better: decision making is more consensual and yields superior results under the new leader Ana's regime. Similarly, in George Romero's *Land of the Dead* (2005), the core group of characters prospers by liberating Slack from her designated role as a prostitute and making her an integral part of the security apparatus. In later seasons of Robert Kirkman's *The Walking Dead* (2010–), the female characters—Michonne, Andrea, and Carol in particular—adopted significant security roles. In the Resident Evil film franchise, the female characters, particularly Alice, seem far more capable of fighting the living dead.* It is no coincidence that, in much of the zombie canon, women make up a disproportionate share of survivors at the end of the narrative.

For liberal feminists, the eradication of gender barriers is both good for world society *and* good for the fight against zombies. Indeed, the only remaining concern for liberal feminists is how the tactics and

---

* I will leave it to future scholarship to explore why there appears to be a positive correlation between the zombie-fighting prowess of the different Resident Evil characters and the extent to which they are costumed in dominatrix gear.

costs of such an approach would be debated in the public sphere. One can envision some feminists urging women to "lean in" to the zombie fight. By pushing hard to occupy scarce leadership positions in the counterzombie apparatus, these leaders can set an example for successive generations of zombie-fighting women. One can also envision critiques to such an approach, bemoaning the difficulty of balancing career ambitions, managing a household, and tending to care relationships with impaling as many flesh-eating ghouls as humanly possible. One can unfortunately envision an endless debate about whether, in a world of the zombie apocalypse, women can "have it all."

Critical feminism would take a more jaundiced view of the effects of the living dead on international society. They would focus on how the zombies would pose serious threats to the disempowered elements of existing society. Manmade disasters can even further marginalize the least powerful elements of society —particularly women.[10] In this atmosphere, feminist critical theorists are trying to find a pathway that retains gender as a category of analysis and the historical commitment to an emancipatory project.[11] One could anticipate a similar dynamic unfolding in the face of the living dead. Consider, for example, the anticipated effects of flesh-eating ghouls on the organization of the state. Priority would inevitably be given to the security apparatus—and these are the

Debates about whether women can "have it all" are likely to
persist during the zombie apocalypse.

areas of political authority that tend to be most exclusionary to women. Even worse, any expansion of
international deployment of security forces would
also lead to a concomitant increase in prostitution

and sex trafficking.[12] This threatens to reify rather than break down preexisting gendered structures. As J. Ann Tickner has observed, "Characteristics associated with femininity are considered a liability when dealing with the realities of international politics."[13] The presence of the living dead, then, could compound subordination based on gender. Critical feminists would express concerns with the securitization caused by the zombie apocalypse and its effect on societies' feminized elements, including women and the poor. While liberal feminists might argue that the exogenous shock of zombies could wrench societies into empowering women, critical feminists would predict that the policy response would subtly shift the status quo in the opposite direction.

We can certainly see the reification of traditional feminine roles in the zombie canon. In Romero's *Night of the Living Dead* (1968), the specter of flesh-eating ghouls completely incapacitates the character of Barbara. She is introduced as a confident, assertive individual in the initial scene of the film. However, after the first zombie attacks she becomes paralyzed with fear and rendered mute for most of the rest of the film. Stripped of her agency, Barbara mostly sits on a couch in a near-catatonic state while the male characters argue about what to do. In both Danny Boyle's film *28 Days Later* (2002) and Brian Keene's novel *The Rising* (2004), we see military troops devote considerable effort to imprisoning women for use as sex slaves. In the first two seasons of Kirkman's *The Walking Dead*, women occupy traditional gendered functions, such as laundry, food preparation, and the education of children. Indeed, at one point Carol tells Laurie that she is the "first lady" of the main survivor group. Only when the group shrinks in size does the gendered division of labor also break down. Later on, Laurie's pregnancy is identified as a driver for the group to find a permanent base in the prison. Numerous conversations among group members about the impracticality of her pregnancy reinforce the notion that traditional feminine tasks are counterproductive in a zombie-infested world. Laurie's subsequent death during childbirth is merely the most obvious reinforcement of this bias. Critical feminists would be profoundly pessimistic about the effects of the living dead and would urge as many precautionary and preventive measures as possible.

Poststructural feminists approach the zombie issue with an even more radical lens, arguing that other feminists are ignoring the importance of intersectionality in identity formation. Poststructuralists highlight that any individual exists at the intersection of multiple mutually altering identities. In a world of intersectionality, international relations is not only heavily gendered but also structured to marginalize issues of race and sexual orientation.[14] A key purpose of such theorizing is to emancipate international relations from its racist, sexist, heteronormative shackles. It is therefore a natural extension to consider whether the introduction of zombies is merely an excuse to segment world society into human and posthuman spheres. Poststructuralists would start their analysis by questioning the ontological need to separate these two groups.

The obvious challenge to the poststructuralist take would be to observe the myriad ways in which the living dead threaten the human order by—oh, you know, eating human beings. Poststructuralists can offer two responses to this objection, however. First, there are examples in the canon of zombies and humans learning to develop intersubjective understandings of each other and, in the process, end the seemingly intractable dispute between them. Perhaps the exemplar of this strain of the zombie literature is Isaac Marion's novel *Warm Bodies* (2011). Written from the perspective of a zombie named R who becomes enamored of a living person named Julie, the novel deftly traces the ways in which both characters develop intersubjective understandings about the other. We learn that the term *corpse* is considered offensive to the zombie community. As R explains, "She is Living and I'm Dead, but I'd like to believe we're both human." Later, as Julie begins to empathize and identify with R, she says, "I mean, isn't 'zombie' just a silly name we came up with for a state of being we don't understand?"[15] Each character begins to question the more negative aspects of his or her group's behavior, such as eating brains or shooting zombies. In the end, zombies evolve and refrain from eating people while the living demilitarize. The theme that love between a living person and a zombie can transcend the constructed differences between the two groups is an example of poststructuralism processes in action.

Second, poststructuralists would argue that it is worth considering the ways in which the living dead could eviscerate gendered structures in modern society. As noted in the chapter "The Social Construction of Zombies," zombies are not constrained by the social construction of gender. A glance at zombie behavior in the canon reveals almost no examples of archetypal gender divisions within that community. Indeed, in many ways the living dead go further, obliterating most biological and sexual differences among the posthuman community. After all, from the undead perspective, the act of procreation is not restricted to women; any zombie can create more zombies. This is not to say that poststructuralists necessarily welcome a zombie apocalypse. Rather, they would argue that by paying attention to the norms that seem to work well within the posthuman sphere, humans could perhaps evolve in ways that negate the reasons for violent conflict in the first place. Post-structuralists offer a way to transcend the traditional debate between liberal feminists and critical feminists in coping with the zombie problem. It might not be a viable way, but it would make for a really interesting social experiment.

A VERY IMPORTANT NOTE ABOUT ZOMBIE NETWORKS

Networks have recently become an important feature of international relations and attending scholarship.[1] A mélange of actors ranging from terrorist groups to social movements to corporate alliances to informal global governance structures appear to have network properties. Scholars are keenly interested in the ways in which social networks affect world politics, and researchers in international relations have used network analysis to model the structure and behavior of these entities. These complex structures are distinguished by the extent to which actors (also called *nodes* in the argot of network analysis) exploit their relationships with other actors (called *ties*). Some networks can be decentralized, in which most nodes have the same number of ties with other nodes. Some networks can be more centralized, however, in which a few key nodes possess the overwhelming share of ties to other actors. The structure of the network can have deep implications for the relative power of participating actors.[2]

Analysts differ in their treatment of networks. Some scholars view the entirety of a network as a single, coherent actor; others view the nodes as the actors, with network ties and structures functioning as constraints on those actors. To date, no scholar has tried to apply network analysis to the living dead, though George Romero's *Diary of the Dead* (2007) was premised on rebooting the story of the zombie apocalypse by telling it, in part, through online social networks.

The first network analysis of zombies will surely be hailed as groundbreaking in the international relations field. The question of whether the hordes of the living dead resemble a random graph more than a power-law distribution of centrality will be addressed. Just as likely, such network analyses will suggest hypotheses, causal mechanisms, and conclusions about the living dead that will be nearly identical to preexisting theoretical approaches that wouldn't recognize a network if they tripped over one in the dark.

NEOCONSERVATISM AND THE AXIS OF EVIL DEAD

In the American foreign policy community, neocon-servatives, or "neocons," are treated as analytically distinct from either realists or liberals. Most interna-tional relations scholars view neoconservative foreign policies as possessing a mélange of liberal and realist tenets, but some believe that this approach represents an altogether different paradigm.[1] On the one hand, neocons agree with liberals about the importance of the democratic peace. Like liberals, neoconservatives believe that a world of democracies would be a more secure global order.[2] They accept the notion that de-mocracies will not fight each other and, therefore, the world is a safer place when there are more democra-cies. Neocons also agree with liberal internationalists that American hegemony contributes to a more just world order.

On the other hand, neoconservatives share the realist skepticism about international institutions.[3] Neocons disdain multilateral institutions as a Nietzs-chian weapon of the weak and the devious.[4] Accord-ing to the neoconservative worldview, international institutions and international law only constrain democracies because of their adherence to the rule of law. Despotic states benefit from cynically embracing multilateralism in theory but not in practice. Neoconservatives do not trust the foreign policy intentions of authoritarian countries. They are also wary of the ability of democratic states to maintain their vigilance in such a dangerous world. Like classical realists, neocons fret about the enervating effects of democracy on the practice of foreign policy.[5]

American neoconservatives are very quick to spot threats and conflicts. In recent years they have articulated many such threats to the American way of life— including those emanating from Russia, China, Iran, North Korea, al-Qaeda, Islam, the European Union, and the United Nations.[6] Provided that the morass of other possible existential threats did not distract them, one would expect neoconservatives to detect the zombie menace at an early stage.*

The neoconservative policy response to an uprising of undead flesh-eaters would be simple and direct. Zombies are an existential threat more serious than any clash of civilizations. To paraphrase Robert Kagan, humans are from Earth and zombies are from Hell.[7] Neither accommodation nor recognition

---

* Indeed, one concern would be that the initial neoconservative response to a zombie outbreak would be to invade Iraq again out of force of habit.

would be sustainable options. The zombies hate us for our freedoms—specifically, our freedom to abstain from eating human brains. As one of the zombies explains in Dan O'Bannon's *Return of the Living Dead* (1985), ghouls eat brains because it is the only thing that eases the pain of being dead.

Neoconservatives would scoff at the realist contention that zombies are like every other actor in world politics and at the liberal contention that global governance structures could cope with the zombie menace. This school of thought would instead recommend an aggressive and militarized response to ensure the continued hegemony of the human race. Rather than wait for the ghouls to come to them, neoconservatives would recommend proactive policy options that would take the fight to the undead. Their policy preference would be for an armed invasion of the central region in the zombie-affected area. Deploying armed forces in ghoul-infested territory would serve two purposes. First, it would act as the zombie equivalent of flypaper, diverting zombies from expanding their dominion. Second, this use of force would eventually drain the swamp of the undead menace.

The neoconservative policy preference on zombies is predicated on the revolution in military affairs permitting swift victory.[8] Based on this military doctrine, neoconservatives would recommend relying on high-tech combat tactics with a heavy focus on air power and special forces to shock and awe the living dead into submission. The hardcore neoconservative position would assert that the use of American power would create a new reality in which the zombies themselves would yearn to break free of their undead state and rejoin the human-based community.[9] Moderate neoconservatives would adopt a more nuanced position; they would posit that, after creating a human outpost in the center of zombie-infested territory, humans in neighboring zombie-afflicted nations would be inspired to rise up and liberate themselves from their undead oppressors. All neoconservatives would welcome a crusade against the undead as worthy of the martial spirit and national greatness that embody the best virtues America has to offer.[10]

It is to neoconservatism's credit that its doctrine is consistent with extant work on how best to respond to the zombie menace.[11] A war against the living dead would, surely, be a war against evil itself.[12] In their counterzombie plan, US Strategic Command explicitly notes the need for "decisive, overwhelming, and possibly unilateral military force" to defeat the undead.[13] However, other elements of neoconservatism might undercut the long-term viability of their initial plans. For example, neoconservatives frequently assume that all adversaries are part of a single axis or alliance of evil enemies. To be sure, that assumption works when confined to zombies, but it is unlikely that neoconservatives would stop there. Because of neoconservative hostility to authoritarianism, they would be inclined to see zombies and despots as part of the same overarching threat. They would inevitably identify reanimated corpses as part of a bigger World War IV against a so-called Axis of Evil Dead that could include Venezuela, Iran, Syria, Hezbollah, Hamas, al-Qaeda, China, and Russia, as well as the combined armies of the undead.[14] Expanding the list of enemies would sabotage any attempt at broad-based coalition warfare, hindering military effectiveness in a global war on zombies.

Furthermore, the military doctrine of shock and awe combined with the light footprint of forces on the ground would prove disastrous in a military campaign against the undead. As Max Brooks noted explicitly in his novel *World War Z* (2006), this doctrine would likely have zero effect on zombies: "[W]hat if the enemy can't be shocked and awed? Not just won't, but biologically *can't*?"[15] Indeed, such a strategy would only trigger a fresh wave of flesh-eating ghouls to rise up. If history is any guide, the initial occupying force would be drawn down too quickly. Over the long run, military forces would likely be enmeshed in a protracted, bloody insurgency from the undead. Indigenous human populations would quickly lose faith in the US military's ability to quell the zombie hordes.

With a massive surge in troops and materiel to clear and hold pockets of zombie-free territory, the neoconservative approach to flesh-eating ghouls might yield modest successes in the long run. The costs, however, would be appalling. The failure of a surge strategy would lead to an inevitable and catastrophic policy response, as demonstrated in Juan Carlos Fresnadillo's *28 Weeks Later* (2007). When a zombie outbreak occurs in the latter half of that film, military forces are quickly given orders to shoot on sight, regardless of whether the person is or isn't infected. Scarlet, a sympathetic army doctor, explains the military mind-set in case of an outbreak of infection: "It all makes sense. They're executing Code Red. Step 1: kill the infected. Step 2: containment. If containment fails, then step 3: extermination." Alas, by the end of that film, despite extreme measures that include the firebombing of London, the zombie infection escapes quarantine and spreads to continental Eurasia.

DOMESTIC POLITICS: ARE ALL ZOMBIE POLITICS LOCAL?

The international relations paradigms discussed to date have been primarily systemic in their orientation.* Their sources of change and explanation in world politics come from the international structure as well as interactions among global actors. While elegant, a systemic approach might miss the more fine-grained power struggles that take place within the confines of domestic politics. The structure of domestic institutions, the state of public opinion, or the constellation of interest group pressures can affect a wide array of foreign policy and national security initiatives. At a minimum, domestic pressures can exert powerful constraints on the foreign policy leader's negotiating tactics and positions when bargaining with other actors.[1]

---

* The key word here is *primarily*. As much as the liberal, realist, and constructivist paradigms might claim to be exclusively systemic in their provenance, all of them dip into both second image (domestic politics) and first image (individuals) at certain points.

The conceptual difficulty with "second image" approaches, however, is their lack of parsimony. Domestic institutions, cultures, and attitudes vary from country to country, making it difficult to boil down differences across borders. Compare and contrast, for example, the reaction to zombies in American movies with the British response in Edgar Wright's *Shaun of the Dead* (2004). Americans tend to display far more visceral reactions, use profanity at a far higher rate, and react quickly and aggressively when a compatriot is bitten. The British tend toward more low-key behavior. Those who are bitten by zombies are reluctant to inform their compatriots about this fact for fear of being a bother. If the United Kingdom and United States are this different in their response to the living dead, imagine how different the variegated national responses of India, Russia, or China might be.

It is difficult to fashion a coherent and parsimonious theory that captures the heterogeneities of each country's domestic politics.[2] To alleviate this problem, this chapter will therefore focus primarily on American and Chinese domestic politics as examples of how second-image factors can affect the global response to an undead uprising. These two countries, as the most powerful in the international system, would profoundly affect any global response to the undead. Furthermore, the national politics of the two countries are sufficiently diverse to illustrate how domestic political approaches can explain outcomes in different settings. The United States is perceived to be a "weak" policy-making state in that the federal government is open to influence from numerous societal interests.[3] The effect of domestic attitudes, interests, and institutions should therefore be most pronounced in the United States, making observation easier. On the other hand, the People's Republic of China is viewed as an institutionalized authoritarian state. Even though new foreign policy actors are emerging on the Chinese stage, their aggregate influence on outcomes is constrained.[4] The effect of domestic interests, and the incentives of politicians in power, will be somewhat different in China than in the United States. This variation in domestic structures permits the observer to weigh the effects of domestic politics on responses to the living dead.

In the United States, would any dimension of domestic politics play a significant role in affecting the global policy response to the emergence of zombies? At first glance, domestic institutions beyond the executive branch would seem to matter little for the zombie issue. The emergence of the living dead poses an immediate threat to homeland security. When faced with such an imminent threat, the executive branch of the government possesses all of the policy levers. The president commands the armed forces, calls up the national guard, and controls a vast intelligence apparatus. The president, and by extension the executive branch, are the agents authorized to negotiate with other countries, expand overseas surveillance, approve covert action, and so forth. For good or ill, in times of catastrophe countervailing institutions such as legislatures and courts play a minimal role during real-time policy formulation and crisis management.[5] To be sure, legislatures can constrain the policy autonomy of the executive branch over time. Even scholars who stress the role of congressional influence acknowledge, however, that a truly global crisis temporarily enhances executive autonomy.[6] Flesh-eating ghouls would surely count as such an exigency.

In theory, public opinion would also not impose an immediate constraint on executive action. At a minimum, one would expect an initial "rally round the flag" phenomenon in response to a zombie emergency.[7] During times of national crisis, populations are inclined to strongly support their national leaders in a display of patriotism. The effect can be long-lasting. Public opinion research shows that Americans would be willing to suffer casualties and costs if they believed in the severity of the national security threat and the likelihood of victory.[8] Provided the initial counterzombie response was sufficiently vigorous, voters would be expected to reward incumbent leaders with greater political support.[9]

Over time, however, public sentiment might impose significant constraints on counterzombie policies. This is particularly true if the source of the undead unrest was far away from the United States. Scholars from Adam Smith onward have observed that mass publics will consider local issues to be far more important than the troubles of foreigners.[10] Indeed, to update a critical passage from book 3, chapter 3 of Smith's *Theory of Moral Sentiments* for our purposes:

Let us suppose that the great empire of China, with all its myriads of inhabitants, was suddenly swallowed up by a plague of the undead, and let us consider how a man of humanity in Europe, who had no sort of connection with that part of the world, would be affected upon receiving intelligence of this dreadful calamity. He would, I imagine, first of all, express very strongly his sorrow for the misfortune of that unhappy people, he would make many melancholy reflections upon the precariousness of human life, as well as the unholy nature of undead existence after the end of life. He would too, perhaps, if he was a man of speculation, enter into many reasonings concerning the effects which this disaster might produce upon the commerce of Europe, and the trade and business of the world in general. And when all this fine philosophy was over, when all these humane sentiments had been once fairly expressed, he would pursue his business or his pleasure, take his repose or his diversion, with the same ease and tranquility, as if no such accident had happened. The most frivolous disaster which could befall himself would occasion a more real disturbance. If he was to lose his little finger to-morrow he would not sleep to-night; but, provided he never saw them, he will snore with the most profound security over the ruin of hundreds of millions of Chinese zombies, and the undead existence of that immense multitude seems plainly an object less interesting to him, than this paltry misfortune of his own. If his finger was bitten off by a flesh-eating ghoul, however, then all bets would be off.

Any effort to combat the zombie problem globally would therefore have to be married to a strong counterzombie effort at home. Even if this was done, one could envision "zombie fatigue" making inroads into public support for overseas operations.* Over time, public sentiment would likely turn against ongoing, far-flung operations that entailed high costs in blood and treasure. This would be true regardless of the foreign policy benefits of such operations. As re-

---

* Public hostility to nationals from zombie-infested countries would be another predicted effect.

Citizens are likely to care more about their own minor discomforts
than they are about a zombie attack in some faraway land.

cent public opinion data suggests, protracted military
conflict, combined with a severe economic recession,
will lead to increased isolationism from the American
masses.[11] Even the most charismatic commander in

chief will encounter the limits of a "press the flesh" strategy when coping with a surly American public.

Interest groups could affect America's domestic and foreign counterzombie policies in multiple ways. There are groups with a vested interest in constraining the eradication of the living dead. The two sets of actors with the most immediate stake in sabotaging any attack on zombies are (1) those who have been bitten by zombies and (2) their human relatives. By definition, when humans are bitten, they will inevitably become zombies. This fact can dramatically alter their preferences. As military planners warned US Strategic Command, "the human instinct for self preservation can cause newly infected zombie hosts to deny their imminent zombification to nearby humans."[12] This change of mind occurs in many zombie films. In George Romero's *Land of the Dead* (2005), the character Cholo has the most militant antizombie attitude at the outset of the film. After he is bitten, however, he decides that he wants to "see how the other half lives." In Peter Jackson's *Dead Alive* (2002), as well as Romero's *Dawn of the Dead* (1978) and *Survival of the Dead* (2010), family members keep their undead relatives hidden from security and paramilitary forces.

Clearly, soon-to-be-ghouls and their relatives can hamper policy implementation. Paradoxically, a failure to implement early measures will force governments to pursue more extreme measures—which, in turn, will be likely to trigger a greater public backlash.

The opening sequences of Romero's *Dawn of the Dead* suggest that one reason the zombie problem spins out of control is public hostility toward harsh government measures and recommendations—martial law, the abandoning of private residences, and the extermination of undead relatives chewing the flesh away from the bones of loved ones.

The soon-to-be-undead and their relatives might hinder policy implementation, but they are too fragmented and ephemeral a grouping to deeply influence the direction of policy making. Defense contractors are another matter entirely. These actors have a significant stake in the allocation of resources devoted to combating zombies. While the idea of a singular, cohesive zombie industrial complex stretches credulity, some corporations in the security sector would undoubtedly be intrigued by the military applications of zombies. In many cases—the films *Return of the Living Dead* (Dan O'Bannon, 1985), *Planet Terror* (Robert Rodriguez, 2007), and *Zombie Strippers* (Jay Lee, 2008) and the Resident Evil franchise—these firms are the very progenitors of the zombie problem. Even if private firms were not the cause of the undead menace, they would no doubt be interested in exploiting the research and development opportunities posed by the reanimation of dead human tissue.

The structural dependence of the state on capital suggests that if the zombie problem were to persist, these firms could impose a more serious constraint on adaptation and mitigation strategies.[13] Corporate pressures on governments to outsource security functions to private contractors—with lucrative contracts, of course—would be intense.[14] Resistance against the elimination of conventional big-ticket military contracts would be fierce. Pharmaceutical companies would lobby for massive subsidies in an effort to develop cures and vaccines for the undead problem—even if such treatments were medically improbable. Defense contractors would resist eradication strategies in favor of approaches that would permit the warehousing and testing of captured ghouls. If firms headquartered in different countries pursued a similar approach, it could provoke a breakdown in trust among nations. Domestic pluralist pressures could sabotage multilateral efforts to stop ghouls from snacking on human flesh.[15]

Obviously, China has a different constellation of domestic public attitudes, institutions, and interests than the United States.[16] This different array of domestic institutions alters China's policy responses to an undead uprising. For one thing, Chinese public opinion, though not completely irrelevant, would matter less in constraining Beijing's response to the living dead. Because China's national leaders do not face democratic elections, their primary concern is about public quiescence, not public preferences. The most powerful Chinese interest groups affecting national policy are the collection of "princelings," children of Chinese

Communist Party officials who have converted their political ties into lucrative businesses.[17] For both personal and political reasons, China's leadership is far more likely to listen to this interest group.

China's authoritarian political institutions make the political incentives of its leadership different from those of democratic politicians. Leaders of such countries have a much smaller fraction of supporters to please than leaders facing democratic electorates. It becomes possible, with such a small "selectorate," for China's leaders to keep their political supporters happy through the transfer of private goods rather than investments in much more expensive public goods.[18] At the same time, the hierarchical political system in China also incentivizes regional leaders to provide overly rosy data to their superiors in Beijing as a pathway to promotion.[19]

How would such a divergent set of second-image politics affect the Chinese response to the living dead? On the one hand, China's political leadership would be less constrained by public reaction in formulating an initial response to the living dead. If flesh-eating ghouls emerge within Chinese territory or in neighboring states, Chinese authorities would be more likely to use all necessary means to eliminate the threat, regardless of the brutality of its tactics or the collateral damage caused by such ruthless counterzombie policies. Chinese authorities would feel no compunction about those costs, provided that such tactics prevented the threat from becoming more widespread. Government officials would also be more willing to censor information about the living dead if doing so would prevent widespread panic.

If the undead problem persisted, however, then the Chinese response would likely become less effective. First, China's central leadership would experience the problem of relying on local proxies to implement orders. As previously noted, such officials might be overly optimistic in their feedback. This would cause the top Chinese leadership to overestimate the effectiveness of its initial counterzombie response. Relatedly, China's regime would also have a greater incentive to allocate more of its counterzombie response to excludable private goods rather than nonexcludable public goods. This would potentially take the form of exclusive redoubts, secure hamlets, and covert exit plans.* These efforts would preserve key political supporters, but at the expense of measures to protect the rest of China's population. In other words, China's leadership would adopt counterzombie policies akin to Kaufman's responses in George Romero's *Land of the Dead* (2005).

---

* To be clear, other countries, including the United States, would also likely see some of these policies to some degree. The difference is that China's leadership would have a political incentive to prioritize these exclusionary policies. In the United States, the wealthy would adopt such measures in a private capacity.

Intriguingly, despite the wide variation in Chinese and American domestic politics, the policy recommendations that come from a domestic politics orientation are relatively straightforward. Clearly, the initial policy responses to a zombie attack are crucial. This is the period when domestic constraints on countermeasures are at their weakest. If governments can fashion clear, coherent, and competent policy actions from the outset, then domestic pressures on policy autonomy should be modest. As a secondary recommendation, governments would be urged to use propaganda and other political tactics to maintain the rally-round-the-flag phenomenon for as long as possible.

If the zombie problem persists, however—through initial policy errors, resistance from entrenched interests, or the logistical difficulties of destroying the undead—then domestic politics will play an increasingly important role in global policy articulation. In democratic countries like the United States, legislatures will slowly exercise more voice, interest groups will constrain policy options, and the public will grow restive toward far-flung operations to eliminate the scourge of the living dead. In more authoritarian countries like China, leaders will over time receive increasingly unreliable information from the provinces, prioritize exit strategies for elites, and direct government policy toward the mass public to focus on the prevention of spontaneous uprisings. If these effects take place across a broad swath of countries, each individual country will find itself more constrained in fashioning a global response. Robert Putnam has talked about how the "two-level games" of domestic and international politics can cause domestic weakness to be translated into international bargaining strength.[20] If all actors face increasing domestic weakness over time, however, then the bargaining core for meaningful international cooperation to combat the undead will slowly rot away.

BUREAUCRATIC POLITICS: THE "PULLING AND HAULING" OF ZOMBIES

All of the aforementioned paradigms share one implicit assumption: that international organizations and national security agencies will act with alacrity and dexterity when the dead start to roam the earth.

This assertion is far from obvious. International organizations often fail to live up to their original founding ideas. Politicized staffing decisions and policy drift can cause these organizations to quickly devolve into dysfunction.[1] Domestic agencies suffer from similar problems.[2] Classic works on bureaucratic politics have modeled foreign and security policies as the outcome of "pulling and hauling" among multiple organizations with different agendas.[3] Other organization theorists argue that political institutions are like "organized anarchies" in which bureaucratic entrepreneurs hawking their solutions are searching for problems rather than the converse.[4] Many political scientists argue that political actors—from the legislative or executive branches—will compromise bureaucratic competence in order to retain political control.[5] The resulting policy outputs are often far from ideal.

Within a single bureaucracy, organizational cultures can constrain flexibility and adaptation to new circumstances. All agencies develop standard operating procedures (SOPs) to efficiently process routine problems.[6] These SOPs, however, can constrain the ability of bureaucracies to adapt to new threats and challenges—and the living dead are anything but a routine problem. The failure of US security and intelligence agencies to reform themselves in the wake of the 9/11 attacks highlights the profound difficulties that bureaucratic politics and organizational cultures can impose on policy making.[7] If bureaucratic conflicts and organizational pathologies hamper effective counterterrorism policies, imagine the effect they would have on counterzombie policies. In their writings, both US Strategic Command and the Centers for Disease Control implicitly assume that they will take the lead in articulating policy. The bureaucratic turf wars would be bloody in every sense of the word.

Quelling the rise of the undead would require significant interagency coordination. In the United States, one could easily envisage major roles for the Departments of State, Defense, Justice, Homeland Security, Transportation, and Health and Human Services. This does not include autonomous or semiautonomous agencies like the Federal Emergency Management Agency, the Environmental Protection Agency,

Bureaucratic turf wars would be bloody in every sense of the word.

the Food and Drug Administration, the Centers for Disease Control and Prevention, and the myriad intelligence agencies. In 2001 Anthony Cordesman estimated that forty-four federal bureaucracies had a hand in combating bioterrorism; it would be safe to assume a similar number would be involved today.[8] Cooperation among the uniformed military, national guard units, and local police and emergency services would also be necessary. Other countries with modern bureaucracies would face similar coordination problems.

Whether bureaucracies can adapt to an army of the undead is an open question. The zombie canon is deeply skeptical about the ability of brainless bureaucrats to handle a problem as deadly as the undead. In Robert Kirkman's series *The Walking Dead* (2010–), the remaining scientists at the Centers for Disease Control and Prevention commit several mistakes, frustrating efforts to understand the pandemic and eventually leading to the destruction of the Atlanta headquarters complex. In Brian Keene's novel *The Rising* (2003), the US government falls apart almost immediately. One trigger is the Secret Service's difficulties altering standard operating procedures. After the president turns into a zombie, he starts devouring the secretary of state. As a result, "one Secret Service agent drew his weapon on the undead Commander-in-Chief, and a second agent immediately shot the first."[9] In divining bureaucratic preferences, where you stand depends on who you eat.

Indeed, the one trait common to every zombie narrative is the ineptitude and fecklessness of bureaucracies. In George Romero's *Night of the Living Dead* (1968), the authorities provide contradictory information to the public: at first they suggest that people stay in their own homes; later they reverse themselves and recommend going to emergency centers. Military officials and scientists are seen bickering on camera about why reanimated corpses are trying to eat people. In Romero's *Dawn of the Dead* (1978), a SWAT raid on a tenement building is executed ineptly, and both civilians and police officers needlessly lose their lives.

Mass desertions within the security services and the disintegration of unit cohesion are recurrent themes in Romero's films. In *Day of the Dead* (1985), the featured team of soldiers and scientists provide a model of organizational dysfunction. The military leader is a near-psychotic, and the leading civilian scientist is little better. A unit goes rogue to blackmail political leaders in *Land of the Dead* (2005). In *Diary of the Dead* (2008), the only time the military makes an appearance is to raid the supplies of civilians. Even researchers on the sociology of panic acknowledge that "the problem with bureaucrats during crises may be the only thing that disaster movies get right."[10]

Max Brooks's work also suggests that both military and civilian agencies would blunder in the wake of zombies. In his novel *World War Z* (2006), one obvious cause of the initial spread of ghouls is the refusal of national security and intelligence bureaucracies in powerful places to acknowledge an "out of the box" problem. When the US Army has its first large-scale engagement with zombies in the Battle of Yonkers, its tactics prove to be completely ill-suited to the situation. Brooks offers a soldier's narrative that encapsulates the organizational pathologies on display:

We wasted so much time, so much energy preparing these elaborate firing positions. Good "cover and concealment" they told us. Cover and concealment? "Cover" means physical protection, conventional protection, from small arms and artillery or air-dropped ordnance. That sound like the enemy we were about to go up against?

And what genius thought to put us in body armor anyway? Because the press reamed 'em for not having enough in the last war? Why the hell do you need a helmet when you're fighting a living corpse?

No one thought about how many rounds the artillery would need for sustained operations....

You think that after being "trained" to aim for the center mass your whole military career you can suddenly make an expert head shot every time?[11]

Each of these statements reveals the inherent difficulties political organizations would have with such a radically new threat. Politics, standard operating procedures, and ingrained modes of thinking would no doubt predominate until such strategies failed to prevent zombies from achieving their goal: feasting upon the flesh of the living.

In earlier work, Brooks identified additional problems that affect the organizational competency and culture of the military: the inevitable logistics and morale gap. "Unlike its human counterparts, an army of zombies is completely independent of support," we read in his *Zombie Survival Guide* (2003). "It will not require food, ammunition, or medical attention. It will not suffer from low morale, battle fatigue, or poor leadership. It will not succumb to panic, desertion, or out-and-out mutiny."[12] Human-run security institutions would undoubtedly confront these problems.

At this point, libertarians no doubt feel secure in their convictions about the rank inefficiency and incompetence of government bureaucracies. It should be noted, however, that private-sector organizations perform just as badly in these narratives. As previously mentioned, for-profit corporations are often responsible for triggering the initial zombie outbreak. In *Dawn of the Dead*, a news station broadcasts out-of-date emergency information to keep up ratings; in *World War Z*, entrepreneurs develop quack remedies for the zombie infection as a way to make a quick profit.

The Resident Evil franchise's Umbrella Corporation is the apotheosis of corporate ineptitude in the zombie canon. While the political power of this multinational corporation is obvious, its organizational competence is highly suspect. In the film series, Umbrella outsources internal security in its research labs to balky and unstable artificial intelligences. Low-ranking employees display minimal loyalty to corporate goals. High-ranking corporate officers make decisions that accomplish little but accelerating the spread of the T-virus farther than intended. This occurs even though the corporation—unique among zombie narratives—already possesses a cure for the undead infection. As a corporate actor, Umbrella's only tangible success appears to be covering its tracks in the mainstream media.

It would seem that flesh-eating ghouls would lead to organizational decision making ranging from the rote to the catastrophic. However, an organizational perspective cannot stop with that first-cut observation. While bureaucracies will inevitably make initial missteps, it would be foolhardy to predict persistent mistakes in the wake of negative feedback. When put under extreme duress, or threatened with extinction, government bureaucracies can adapt and overcome. Indeed, the failure to recognize this possibility is the biggest blind spot in the zombie canon. If humans can think faster than zombies, then their greatest comparative advantage in a future conflict will be their ability to develop innovative tactics and strategies. Some long-running zombie stories presume the evolution of zombies. Curiously, however, very few of them discuss how human individuals and organizations would adapt.

World War Z provides the best example of human adaptation. After the disaster at the Battle of Yonkers, the military begins to alter its doctrine. Most major

governments quickly adopt a grand strategy of securing a geographically well-defined safe zone; US forces
retreat to the west side of the Rocky Mountains. The
new chairman of the Joint Chiefs of Staff develops
the "resource-to-kill ratio" (RKR) in order to maxi-
mize military efficiency. In the process, there are some
clear bureaucratic losers,[13] but the stress of scarcity
forces a rationalization of resources. As one character
recounts in Brooks's narrative, "What was so amazing
to see was how the culture of RKR began to take hold
among the rank and file. You'd hear soldiers talking
on the street, in bars, on the train; 'Why have X, when
for the same price you could have ten Ys, which could
kill a hundred times as many Zs.' Soldiers even began
coming up with ideas on their own, inventing more
cost-effective tools than we could have envisioned."[14]

An organizational perspective would therefore
predict that government agencies would misstep and
err at the initial stages of a zombie attack. This same
perspective would also argue that ecological pressure
on these organizations to survive and thrive would
lead to adaptation and improvisation. This prediction
is probabilistic, however. In Juan Carlos Fresnadillo's
28 Weeks Later (2007), for example, a NATO expedi-
tionary force reoccupies Great Britain after the "rage
virus" has exterminated the population. Even though
the commanders are fully aware of the dangers of infection, they abjectly fail to prevent its reemergence.

The policy recommendations that a bureaucratic politics perspective offers are straightforward and consist largely of ways to avoid the worst organizational pathologies and turf wars. No doubt the battle over which agency or bureaucracy would have the "lead" over how to defeat the undead would be fierce. National governments should consider designating a lead agency before rather than after flesh-eating ghouls start chomping on citizens. In Mira Grant's *Feed* (2010), for example, the Centers for Disease Control and Prevention becomes the lead agency, amassing considerable amounts of operational and security capabilities in the process.

Perhaps the organizational perspective's strongest recommendation would be to exploit technologies that flatten organizational hierarchies and make information more readily available. It is disconcerting to note that despite US Strategic Command's development of a counterzombie plan in 2011, the Chairman of the Joint Chiefs of Staff was unaware of the plan's existence two years later. This may be a result of the military's rigid hierarchy. Networked structures have the capacity to collect and disseminate information more quickly. If both national and international organizations relied on flatter arrangements, information from operators about the resilience of the undead can move up the hierarchy as soon as possible. This would accelerate rapid responses to zombie emergencies, and allow the best counterzombie tactics and strategies to diffuse across the globe.[15]

There is a tragic irony to these predictions and recommendations. Recall the discussion of how domestic politics would affect counterzombie policies: government institutions would be able to act in an unconstrained manner at first, but politics would impose a stronger constraint over time. The organizational perspective offers the reverse narrative—bureaucratic competency will improve over time. If both domestic political pressures and bureaucratic politics play a role in affecting government policies, their combined effect could be doubly disastrous. Government agencies would have the most autonomy when they are most likely to make bad decisions. By the time these bureaucracies adapted to new zombie exigencies, they would face political hurdles that could hamper their performance.

WE'RE ONLY HUMAN: PSYCHOLOGICAL RESPONSES TO THE UNDEAD

Zombies are often assumed to lack intelligence, but it should be noted that humans frequently respond to new undead situations with confusion and ignorance. Indeed, even a cursory glance at human behavior in the zombie canon highlights puzzling or seemingly irrational actions on the part of the human characters. In Edgar Wright's *Shaun of the Dead* (2004), the protagonists insist that safety can be found in the local pub even though it is located in a densely populated urban area. In Ruben Fleischer's *Zombieland* (2009), some of the characters are oddly certain that a Disney-style theme park will be zombie-free. In George Romero's *Dawn of the Dead* (1978), marauding bikers pelt zombies with cream pies, acting as if that will incapacitate them. In Dan O'Bannon's *Return of the Living Dead* (1985), the zombies are smarter than most of the human characters. In an episode of Robert Kirkman's TV series *The Walking Dead* (2010–), The Governor conducts assaults on Rick's group in the prison in a manner devoid of any tactical or strategic logic. Failing in his first assault, he kills most of his supporters, burns down an effective compound in Woodbury, and then stumbles upon another group of survivors—at which point he repeats his ill-advised assault on the prison. There is no shortage of stupid or self-defeating behavior in the zombie canon. Or, as Colson Whitehead observed in *Zone One*, "you had to watch out for other people. The dead were predictable. People were not."[1]

This should not be surprising. A zombie outbreak is perfectly designed to prey on powerful emotions—fear, disgust, revulsion, and dread—that can cause deviations from prudential behavior.[2] Zombies occupy the lowest depths of the "uncanny valley" of human likenesses, which means that they resemble humans enough to trigger instant disgust and revulsion.[3] The spread of zombies encapsulates the elements of an epidemic that should arouse the greatest amount of dread and anxiety from individuals. Fear and suspicion are much more severe in their effects when the source of danger is new, as any review of first reactions to AIDS, severe acute respiratory syndrome (SARS), or the H1N1 swine flu will reveal.[4]

The canonical responses to the zombie threat suggest that human beings cannot be reduced to bloodless calculating machines despite the assumptions of rational choice theorists. All individuals have fears, foibles, and failings that cause behavior to deviate from how a dispassionate decision maker would behave. First-image theorists look at these tendencies in human behavior and see whether they translate into recurrent patterns in world politics.[5]

There are a cluster of cognitive attributes hard-wired into all humans that might affect policy responses to an uprising of the living dead. Perhaps the most powerful is the tendency for *confirmation bias* in processing new information about a phenomenon.[6] All individuals have ideologies, cognitive heuristics, or rules of thumb they use to explain how the world works. When confronted with an unusual or anomalous event, most people will focus on the bits of information that correspond to their preconceived worldviews. They will use historical analogies to guide their actions—even if these analogies are imperfect.[7] At the same time, they will ignore or suppress information that contradicts their beliefs. Only if their preconceived ideas lead to radical policy failures will most individuals be willing to rethink their worldviews.

Indeed, confirmation bias helps to explain why first responders would likely fail to halt an initial zombie outbreak. Preventive action would require these people to logically conclude that the dead are walking the earth—a fact that contradicts most logocentric worldviews. As Jonathan Maberry observes, "the zombie has to be seen and identified as a disease-carrying hostile vector. That's not going to happen quickly or easily, and probably not at all during this [early] phase."[8] Max Brooks is even more emphatic on this point: "Governments of any type are no more than a collection of human beings—human beings as fearful, short-sighted, arrogant, closed-minded, and generally incompetent as the rest of us. Why would they be willing to recognize and deal with an attack of walking, bloodthirsty corpses when most of humanity isn't?"[9]

A prominent form of confirmation bias in international relations is *fundamental attribution error*. When interpreting the behavior of other actors, individuals will often treat allies and adversaries in different ways.[10] If an ally does something positive, individuals will attribute this behavior to his internal character. If an adversary acts in a constructive manner, however, that is attributed to pressures by the external environment —that is, he was forced into being good. Conversely, if an ally acts in an unproductive manner, that is explained away as a situation in which external circumstances forced a good actor to behave badly. If an adversary acts in the same manner, however, then it is because he is inherently wicked.

Another type of behavioral trait common to individual decision makers is their tendency to act differently when confronted with gains or losses relative to the status quo.[11] Rational choice theory assumes that individuals have constant attitudes toward risk. According to *prospect theory*, however, people tend to be more risk averse when operating in a world of gains, and more risk loving when operating in a world of losses. To use some numerical examples, imagine you face the following choice:

Option A: The certain destruction of 500 zombies

Option B: A 50 percent chance of destroying 1,000 zombies and a 50 percent chance of destroying 100 zombies

In a July 2010 online survey that yielded 1,238 respondents, I found that more than 61 percent chose option A, even though option B offered the greater expected value of destroyed ghouls. Indeed, numerous experiments demonstrate that when individuals have to choose between a guaranteed prize and a lottery offering a prize with a slightly higher expected value, they will take the sure thing.

Now, consider a different choice:

Option A: A certain increase of 500 zombies

Option B: A 50 percent chance of creating only 100 new zombies and a 50 percent chance of creating 1,000 new zombies

In this case, more than 57 percent of respondents chose option B, even though the expected value of option A is better. If people must choose between a sure loss or a lottery in which the expected value is worse but the possibility exists of returning to the status quo, they will gamble for resurrection.

The policy implications of prospect theory are clear. Compared to the status quo, individuals will act in a more cautious, risk-averse manner when they believe that they are gaining ground. When they perceive themselves to be losing ground, individuals will be more willing to take risky gambits in an effort to resuscitate their fortunes.[12]

First-image theorists argue that this cluster of psychological attributes leads to a "hawk bias" in foreign affairs.[13] When confronted with a possible adversary, the psychological response by individual policy makers will lead to more confrontational policies. Aggressive actions will be interpreted as intentional. When threatened with a possible loss, policy makers will be more willing to take risky actions to preserve the status quo. Other psychological traits—such as optimism bias and the illusion of control—will reinforce aggressive policies.[14] Leaders will be supremely confident that proactive measures can address whatever threat emerges from beyond the grave.

Oddly enough, while the hawk bias might be a bad fit for human international relations, it would provide the right frame of mind for how to respond to flesh-eating ghouls. The revulsion caused by zombies would make it easy for individuals to label them as the enemy. Confirmation bias would ensure that any new data about zombies would simply reinforce their enemy status. Prospect theory would guarantee that leaders, when faced with initial losses from undead attacks, would double down with risky strategies designed to reclaim the status quo. The hawk bias might exaggerate conflict with humans, but it would appear to promote just the right attitude toward the living dead.

The zombie canon suggests two important caveats to this generally positive assessment, however. First, confirmation bias and fundamental attribution error will also lead individuals to treat their zombified relatives differently than others. As previously noted, a staple of the canon is for people to refrain from killing relatives who turn into flesh-eating ghouls. In Romero's *Survival of the Dead*, (2010) for example, one family patriarch refuses to kill any zombie in his clan, arguing that it would be tantamount to "killing our own kind." Some individuals in the canon also suffer from optimism bias and the illusion of control. For example, in Kirkman's *The Walking Dead*, Herschel is convinced that the zombies can be cured and therefore should not be killed. The living dead would exploit this misperception, allowing the army of zombies to increase through an undead form of social networking. Family members would infect other family members, friends would infect friends, and so forth.

Second, it is unclear whether the perceptual response to zombies would be limited just to the undead. It is highly likely that the hawk bias would cause individuals to distrust and fear other humans as well. In situations of flux, it would be easy to envisage humans accusing other humans of being bitten by a zombie on the basis of flimsy evidence. This internecine conflict among humans—and among human governments—could paralyze efforts to maintain a common counterzombie front.

First-image models would provide three concrete policy recommendations to combat the scourge of the living dead. First, it will be crucial for governments and international organizations to quickly and effectively proffer new rules and methods for coping with the undead. Individuals can adapt quickly to new circumstances, provided that those circumstances provide for some stability over time.[15] If individuals know what the "new normal" looks like during a zombie outbreak, panic will be much less widespread.

Second, policies should be implemented that "nudge" individuals into pursuing the right kind of counterzombie tactics.[16] These policies should have default options that lead to prudential counterzombie behavior rather than assuming that individuals will adopt their own active counterzombie measures. For example, after a zombie attack, a new component of any driver's license exam might be a demonstration of evasion tactics—or how to perform a hit-and-run on a flesh-eating ghoul with minimal damage to the motor vehicle.

There is one final, risky gambit—but it just might work. This chapter has focused on the psychological attributes of humans—but what about the psychology of zombies? One of the biggest puzzles in the zombie studies literature is why the living dead are compelled to devour humans even though there appears to be no biological reason for flesh-eating activity.[17] Given the tendency of zombies to travel in packs and mobs, first-image theorists would hypothesize that this decision to eat humans is a classic case of *groupthink*, the tendency for individuals to prioritize group consensus over a thorough vetting of alternative ideas and proposals.[18] This phenomenon has been observed in humans, but perhaps it explains zombie behavior as well. Based on their grouping behavior, it could be argued that the living dead care the most about reaching a consensus among themselves about their social purpose. This could lead individual zombies not to question the assumptions behind the decision to eat humans.

A risky but intriguing policy option would be for human governments to use psychological operatives to engage in "cognitive infiltration" of the undead community. Such efforts have already been proposed for extremist and terrorist groups.[19] Through suggestive grunting, moaning, and shrugging, perhaps these operatives could end the epistemic closure among zombies and get them to question their ontological assumptions. If zombies threw off their cognitive shackles and recognized that they did not need to eat

Placing undercover operatives in a zombie horde would be a
high-risk, high-reward strategy.

human beings, then the crisis of the undead would be
much less severe.

Of course, it is also possible that the living dead
would devour the agents before they could perform
their tasks. As prospect theory suggests, however, desperate times lead to desperate measures.

CONCLUSION
. . . OR SO YOU THINK

A specter is haunting world politics—the specter of reanimated corpses coming to feast on people's brains. To date, the scholarly response from international relations theory to the zombie menace has been only skin-deep. I have tried to take a much deeper cut at this looming problem. As the preceding pages should make clear, international relations theory offers some interesting and varied predictions and recommendations about how governments, international institutions, domestic interests, bureaucracies, and individuals would respond to the transnational threat posed by the living dead.

A quick review reveals some interesting continuities across the different theoretical paradigms. For example, most of these approaches would predict that the living dead would have an unequal effect on different national governments. Powerful states would be more likely to withstand an army of flesh-eating ghouls. Weaker and developing countries would be more vulnerable to a zombie infestation. Whether due to realist disinterest, discriminatory policies toward women, waning public support, bureaucratic wrangling, or the fallibility of individual decision makers, international interventions would likely be ephemeral or imperfect. Complete eradication of the zombie menace would be extremely unlikely. The plague of the undead would join the roster of threats that disproportionately affect the poorest and weakest countries.

The different theories also provide a greater variety of possible outcomes than the bulk of the zombie canon. Traditional zombie narratives in film and fiction are quick to get to the apocalypse. Most of the theoretical approaches presented here, however, suggest that there would be a vigorous policy response to the menace of the living dead. Realism posits an eventual live-and-let-live arrangement between the undead and everyone else. Liberals predict an imperfect but useful counterzombie regime. Neoconservatives believe that an aggressive and thorough military deployment would keep the undead menace at bay. Some constructivists would predict a robust pluralistic security community dedicated to preventing new zombie outbreaks and socializing existing zombies into human society. Poststructuralist feminists would posit a world without distinctions between humans and posthumans. Organizations might err in their initial response, but they could also adapt and overcome. Individuals would be hardwired toward an aggressive policy response against the living dead. These kinds of predictions suggest that maybe, just maybe, the zombie canon's dominant narrative of human extinction is overstated.

While encouraging, this survey also reveals some cautionary warnings lurking on the horizon. First, catastrophic outcomes are still quite possible. Bureaucratic dysfunction could trigger a total collapse in state authority. Public opinion and interest group pressure could make multilateral cooperation more difficult. A norm cascade could trigger a world in which the biological distinctions between humans and zombies would be immaterial—everyone would act like zombies. Policy makers or individuals could overreact against the zombie menace, killing many humans in the process. Still, these are *possible* outcomes; whether they are the *likely* outcomes is another question altogether.

Second, from a human security perspective, even the "optimistic" outcomes discussed above would be unmitigated disasters compared to the prezombie state of the world. Human security approaches focus on risks to individuals, whereas national security approaches focus on risks to states.[1] From this perspective, anything that threatens an individual's bodily integrity qualifies as a threat. In a world in which zombies were concentrated in the poorest and weakest countries, billions of human beings would have an additional threat to contend with on top of disease, poverty, and the erosion of the rule of law. A majority of the world's population would not achieve freedom from fear in a world where the undead roam.

This sobering assessment highlights a flaw in the standard international relations paradigms—their eroding analytical leverage over the security problems of the twenty-first century. Most international relations theories are state-centric, but interstate conflict is not as significant a threat anymore. Indeed, despite widespread perceptions to the contrary, there has been a significant and secular decline in interstate violence over the past few centuries.[2] Consider the list of dangers that opened this book; almost none of them emanated from states. Neither terrorists nor hackers possess large swaths of territory, making retaliation difficult. Natural disasters like earthquakes or volcanoes do not possess "agency" as we understand the concept; neither do disease vectors or melting glaciers. The international relations profession has always started with the state—and governments will continue to be an important part of the world politics equation. Unless these theories can adapt to the plethora of asymmetric threats to the human race, however, they will be hard-pressed to offer cogent policy responses to the living dead.

Clearly, further research is needed. This leads to some final but crucial questions: How can we assess the explanatory power of each paradigm's predictions? Is only one of them true? Some of them? All of them? In the social sciences, the best way to adjudicate among different theories is to devise empirical tests that buttress or falsify the different approaches. For the zombie question at hand, however, that is neither desirable nor plausible.

The international relations scholar must concede that analytical rigor alone is an insufficient basis for political judgment on how to respond to the living dead. A paradigmatic approach to explaining political outcomes provides some useful analytical tools, but the tool kit remains incomplete. Even international relations theorists themselves are aware of this fact. Perhaps individual realists would treat zombies as different from humans; perhaps advocates of legislative constraints would allow that an attack from the living dead might overwhelm Congress's ability to respond. It is possible that, when confronted with a concrete policy problem like flesh-eating ghouls, specific microtheories—contingent hypotheses that apply to a very narrow set of circumstances—might be more useful than the grand paradigms.[3]

Having the judgment to know which models apply in world politics—and when—is more art than science.[4] As Albert Hirschman observed soon after George Romero's *Night of the Living Dead* (1968) was released, "[O]rdinarily social scientists are happy enough when they have gotten hold of *one* paradigm or line of causation. As a result, their guesses are often further off the mark than those of the experienced politician whose intuition is more likely to take a variety of forces into account."[5]

This volume serves as a caution against the fallacious but prevalent view of zombie studies: that the world will end once the dead walk the earth. It is up to readers to exercise their own judgment in determining what to do with that information. International relations theory clearly retains some practical utility. Perhaps, however, the ability of these theories to explain current global threats and challenges is more circumscribed than international relations theorists proclaim in their scholarship. Informed by these paradigms, the interested and intelligent students of world politics should use their own brains to cogitate on this question—before the zombies decide to use them instead.

EPILOGUE:
BRINGING THE BRAIN BACK IN

By any observable metric, the living dead have become an even hotter pop culture phenomenon since
the publication of the first edition of *Theories of International Politics and Zombies*. The pace of zombie
movie production had accelerated, and the 2013
film version of *World War Z* grossed more than half
a billion dollars worldwide. Robert Kirkman's AMC
series *The Walking Dead* has become a ratings powerhouse, inspiring the development of like-minded
shows. A running joke on Fox's *The New Girl* to demonstrate one character's lack of career ambition is
his unfinished zombie novel, *Z Is for Zombie*.[1] By any
metric of scholarly output, research on zombies has
exploded.[2] Why do the living dead continue to ride
so high in the cultural sky? And, frankly, is this good
for the humans?

To appreciate the zombie's longer-than-fifteen
minutes in the pop culture spotlight, one has to start
by revisiting the arguments presented here. Zombies occupy what roboticists and animators call "the
uncanny valley" in human perception—so close to
being human, and yet decidedly not human, that they
prompt instant revulsion. Furthermore, one commonality to all zombie narratives is that 100 percent

of the people bitten by zombies will eventually turn into zombies. Even the most virulent pathogens encountered in the real world—Ebola or HIV—have infection rates below 50 percent.

These "dreaded risk" qualities matter,[3] because there is a correlation between zombie movie production and times of war, recession, pandemics, or general unhappiness. And even as traditional international security threats are waning, nontraditional threats seem to assault the senses constantly. Concerns about terrorism have not abated since the September 11, 2001, attacks, despite the actual decline in terrorist attacks. Drug-resistant pandemics have been a staple of local news hysteria since the H1N1 swine flu swept across the United States in 2009. Scientists continue to warn about the dangers that climate change poses to our planet. If 2008 taught anything, it is that crisis and contagion are endemic to the global financial system. In 2013, US officials announced that cyberattacks were now the top national security threat. The spread of seemingly unpredictable and spontaneous uprisings, from the Arab Spring in 2011 to Russia in 2012 to Brazil and Turkey in 2013 to Ukraine and Venezuela in 2014, feed a sense that political order is more fragile.

The threats to national security are less grave but provoke more uncertainty than during the Cold War. Zombies are the perfect symbol to represent these threats in popular culture. Much like pandemics or financial crises, it is impossible to negotiate with the living dead. Similar to online or offline terrorism, it seems like just a small outbreak of flesh-eating ghouls can wreak massive carnage. And a mob of reanimated, ravenous corpses is as inexorable a force as climate change.

Elite appropriation of zombies has further reified their cultural significance. Because the living dead resonate so strongly in the current cultural zeitgeist, it should not be surprising that various provocateurs and policy entrepreneurs use the living dead as a "hook" for their own ideas. It seems impossible for the *New York Times* op-ed page to go a week without a contributor bringing up zombies.[4] The living dead are now standard fare in commercials advertising products ranging from cell phones to politicians. REI has marketed "13 Essential Tools for Surviving a Zombie Outbreak"—each available for purchase at its retail stores. The annual Zombie Safe House Competition challenges architects to design the best ghoul-proof home.[5]

Agencies of the US federal government have been the savviest at exploiting the living dead. In May 2011, the US Centers for Disease Control and Prevention posted a small item on one of its blogs about what to do if the dead should rise from the grave to feast upon the entrails of the living.[6] Within two hours it went viral, and the CDC's web server crashed from the upsurge in traffic. Recognizing a good thing, the CDC soon released *Zombie Preparedness 101*, a comic book designed to educate readers in how to prepare against a zombie attack—which, not coincidentally, requires the same steps as preparing for natural disasters.[7]

Other federal agencies have picked up on the CDC's success. The Department of Homeland Security also incorporated zombies into its planning and publicity operations. Most prominently, US Strategic Command produced a contingency plan for counter-zombie dominance. In their opening, the authors explained, "the hyperbole involved in writing a 'zombie survival plan' actually provided a very useful and effective training tool."[8] Governments outside the United States have also embraced the zombie trope as a way to promote disaster preparedness.

These examples highlight the positive ways that the living dead can be expropriated as a metaphor to spark interest in other ideas. One of the strengths of the horror genre is that it allows people to talk about present-day problems without addressing them straight-on. Instead of droning on about the specter of climate change, one can highlight the problem by changing the threat to the living dead. The moment zombies are added into the mix, an abstruse public policy problem suddenly becomes a rollicking argument accessible to ordinary citizens. USSTRATCOM agreed, noting at the outset of their plan, "if you suspend reality for a few minutes, this type of training scenario can actually take a very dry, monotonous topic and turn it into something rather enjoyable."[9] Drawing from popular culture also allows for greater creativity in the response to new challenges or new situations. Indeed, the very act of referencing fiction encourages policy entrepreneurs to use their narrative imagination to tackle problems in unorthodox and fruitful ways.

Still, constant references to the living dead in popular culture also have problematic features. This became clear after a bizarre attack in May 2012 in Miami, in which one man tried to eat another man's face and was not easily subdued despite multiple gunshots from police. The Miami attack triggered a massive spike in Google searches for "zombie apocalypse." After the attack, the CDC was forced to publicly deny the existence of a zombie virus.[10] Documentaries about zombies have suggested that the attack could be a government research effort gone awry.

As was discussed in the chapter "The Zombie Literature," beliefs in the paranormal have a viral quality: sociological research suggests that exposure to other people's beliefs increase the likelihood of accepting that same belief regardless of its plausibility. The more that zombies bleed from their own subgenre into the mainstream media, the more people will believe that they could actually exist. In other words, you people reading this epilogue are part of the problem.

An even more serious problem is the weakness of analogies.[11] Policy entrepreneurs have understandably piggybacked on zombies to capture attention. The idea behind analogical reasoning is that if the initial conditions of a threat seem to match those of flesh-eating ghouls, this will prompt acute policy responses. This is all well and good but misses a key fact about zombie stories—their depressing homogeneity. In almost all of them, the living dead are introduced in minute one. By minute ten, the world is a postapocalyptic wasteland. The implication is that if zombielike threats emerge, both the state and civil society will break down.

Interest in the living dead has shifted from a focus on *zombies* to a focus on the *zombie apocalypse*. The television shows that been inspired by AMC's *The Walking Dead* do not necessarily have zombies, but rather a postapocalyptic setting. Such shows include TNT's *Falling Skies* and *The Last Ship*, NBC's *Revolution*, and FX's *The Strain*, as well as National Geographic's reality show *Doomsday Preppers*. Similarly, Marc Forster's film *World War Z* premiered in the summer of 2013, when the end of the world was also captured in Joseph Kosinski's *Oblivion*, Guillermo del Toro's *Pacific Rim*, M. Night Shyamalan's *After Earth*, Evan Goldberg and Seth Rogen's *This Is the End*, and

Edgar Wright's *The World's End*. It is not just zombies that have crested culturally—it is the end of the world.

One could argue that all of this belongs in the realm of escapism. Apocalypse narratives matter, however, if people implicitly accept the notion that some threats will actually trigger a societal breakdown. Perception plays an important role in maintaining national resilience and public order. If citizens *think* that we're teetering on the brink of chaos, the apocalyptic mind-set can, in and of itself, help bring about the very thing it perceives.

There is at least some prima facie evidence that doomsday prepping has already influenced policy debates in the United States. In the wake of the December 2012 shooting tragedy in a Newtown, Connecticut, school, National Rifle Association executive vice president Wayne LaPierre stridently opposed any proposed gun regulations, which is unsurprising. What is surprising is his millenarian explanation for that position:

> Hurricanes. Tornadoes. Riots. Terrorists. Gangs. Lone criminals. These are perils we are sure to face—not just maybe. It's not paranoia to buy a gun. It's survival. It's responsible behavior, and it's time we encourage law-abiding Americans to do just that....

> Responsible Americans realize that the world as we know it has changed. We, the American people, clearly

see the daunting forces we will undoubtedly face: terrorists, crime, drug gangs, the possibility of Euro-style
debt riots, civil unrest or natural disaster.

Gun owners are *not* buying firearms because they anticipate a confrontation with the government. Rather, we
anticipate confrontations where the government isn't
there—or simply doesn't show up in time.[12]

In essence, LaPierre's argument was that the current state of the world is so apocalyptic that it is rational for individual citizens to prepare for the end
of days. This is particularly odd given that the evidence shows a sustained decline in both violent crime
and property crime in the United States.[13] Lest one
dismiss such hyperbole to interest-group lobbying,
senator Lindsey Graham also worried aloud about
inadequate firepower if, say, "chemicals have been released into the air and law enforcement is really not
able to respond and people take advantage of that
lawless environment."[14] When lobbyists and senators
muse aloud about a *Return of the Living Dead* scenario,
there's a problem with the state of political discourse.
Indeed, in response to a Florida bill that would have
allowed residents to carry firearms without a con-
cealed weapon permit during times of emergency;
a state senator proposed amending the bill's title to
read "an act relating to the zombie apocalypse."[15] The
renaissance of the zombie in popular culture may be

in and of itself feeding a cultural zeitgeist that assumes society will be collapsing at any moment—in direct contradiction of all long-term data suggesting the exact opposite.[16]

Is there a cure to our millenarian cul-de-sac that does not, following the constructivist policy option, obliterate the entire zombie canon? The solution, perhaps, is the infusion of more creative zombie narratives. There will always be a place in zombie lore for the grim, unrelentingly dour postapocalyptic visions of George Romero, and of Robert Kirkman's series *The Walking Dead* (2010–). That said, popular culture also needs more narratives like Max Brooks's *World War Z* (2006), Isaac Marion's *Warm Bodies* (2011), or even Steven Soderbergh's *Contagion* (2012), in which the adaptability, ingenuity, and creativity of human beings is also put on full display. One of the most important conclusions of this book is that most of the zombie canon underestimates the ability of human beings to adapt more quickly than any nonhuman threat. Any species that invented duct tape, smartphones, and Twinkies stands a better-than-fighting chance against the living dead. Narratives about flesh-eating ghouls should still be scary, but they can also remind audiences that humans have an enormous capacity to adapt to new threats and overcome them. We will only learn to combat the policy problems created by the metaphor of the living dead by bringing the brain back in.

ACKNOWLEDGMENTS
TO THE FIRST EDITION

Growing up I was not a fan of the horror movie genre. My earliest memory of a horror film was watching ten minutes of *Poltergeist* as a kid and then not sleeping that night. It wasn't until I stumbled across *28 Days Later* one night on television that I developed any enjoyment for the zombie genre. I am therefore grateful to Danny Boyle and Alex Garland, the director and writer of that underrated film, for getting me interested in zombie flicks in the first place.

The genesis of this monograph was a *Foreign Policy* blog entry that I posted in August 2009.* The post garnered a fair amount of attention within both the blogosphere and the international relations community. A number of international relations professors contacted me to say that they had directed their students to this post because it provided an accessible entry point into the more abstruse areas of international relations theory. This inspired me to see if the premise could be expanded into what you are now reading.

*Daniel W. Drezner, "Theory of International Politics and Zombies," *Foreign Policy*, August 18, 2009, http://drezner.foreign policy.com/posts/2009/08/18/theory_of_international_politics_ and_zombies (accessed July 15, 2010).

I thank Alex Massie for piquing my interest about the zombie question with his blog post on the topic. At *Foreign Policy*, Rebecca Frankel, Susan Glasser, Blake Hounshell, Joshua Keating, Moises Naim, Britt Peterson, and Tom Stec have provided me a wonderful home at which to blog about everything from arcane disputes within international relations theory to the global governance of movie apocalypses. A portion of this manuscript was excerpted in the July–August 2010 issue of *Foreign Policy*.*

Chanda Phelan was kind enough to provide me with her data on postapocalyptic fiction.

I foisted the draft manuscript onto more friends, family members, colleagues, and complete strangers than I do my more conventional work. I thank Bethany Albertson, Kyle Brownlie, Charli Carpenter, Stephanie Carvin, Jonathan Caverley, Sam Crane, Erika Drezner, Esther Drezner, Shohreh Harris, Charlie Homans, John Horgan, Patrick Thaddeus Jackson, Jacob T. Levy, Kate McNamara, Blake Messer, Micah Mintz, Jennifer Mitzen, Dan Nexon, Negeen Pegahi, Gabriel Rossman, Steve Saideman, Anna Seleny, Joanne Spetz, Laurie Wilkie, Jason Wilson, and Amy Zegart for their feedback, advice, and support. Whether they knew it or not, Alan Beattie, Elizabeth

*Daniel W. Drezner, "Night of the Living Wonks," *Foreign Policy* 180 (July–August 2010): 34–38.

Economy, Brad Gendell, Yfat Reiss Gendell, Jennifer M. Harris, G. John Ikenberry, David Lake, and Michael Mastanduno provided useful suggestions.

The team at Princeton University Press has dramatically improved this book with their meticulousness, energy, and professionalism. I am grateful to Julia Livingston, Natalie Baan, Theresa Liu, and Jennifer Roth for their assistance in converting this book from pixels to print. Brian Bendlin saved me from many abstruse errors with his copyediting. Each of Anne Karetnikov's drawings are worth a thousand words—which means she's responsible for an awful lot of the intellectual value of this book. Political science editor Chuck Myers and editor in chief Peter Dougherty will have my eternal, undying gratitude for being brave enough to think, "Why yes, now that we think about it, what's really missing from our catalog is a book on international relations and zombies."

My wife Erika reacted to this book idea in the same way she reacts to all of my ideas—with an appropriate mixture of reassurance and bemusement. My appreciation for her unstinting, level-headed support in these endeavors will last well beyond the grave.

Finally, to Kenneth Waltz, author of *Theory of International Politics*, an icon in my field of study, and someone whom I've never properly met: I'm very sorry.

ACKNOWLEDGMENTS
TO THE REVIVED EDITION

There would be no revived edition of this book without the encouragement and support of Princeton University Press. I am grateful to Eric Crahan at the Press for pushing me to revise and update the book. Brian Bendlin revived his job as copy editor to improve the prose, and Anne Karetnikov added more stellar illustrations to the mix.

Many colleagues helped me in the preparation of additional material for this second edition. The epilogue is a revised and expanded version of an essay that first appeared in the *Wall Street Journal*.* I thank Gary Rosen for giving me the opportunity to write that essay, and Lenny Simmons for letting me play with those ideas at a TEDx conference, "Sex, Tech and Rock & Roll" in Binghamton, New York. I leaned on a lot of colleagues for advice and feedback for the feminist theory chapter; many thanks to Charli Carpenter, Stephanie Carvin, Nancy Hite, Laura McKenna, Kate McNamara, Laura Sjoberg, and Mariah Zeisberg for making that chapter a much better piece of scholarship.

*Daniel W. Drezner, "The Lessons of Zombie-Mania," *Wall Street Journal*, April 6, 2013.

Finally, there would have been no revived edition without the success of the first edition—and for that, there are other people to thank. My publicist for the first edition, Whitney Peeling, did a fantastic job in helping me to promote the book. I owe a debt to my fellow members of the Zombie Research Society advisory board—particularly Max Brooks, Matt Mogk, Steve Schlozman, Timothy Verstynen, and Brad Voytek—for reassuring me that I was not alone in writing about the living dead. I am thankful to everyone who attended my talks at ZomBcon, Walker-Stalker Con, and Comic-Con, for showing me that there was an untapped audience for such scholarship. Most of all, however, I am grateful to all the international relations professors who have assigned my book in their classes. The goal of this project has always been to make the reader laugh and think—though not necessarily in that order. Based on the feedback I've received from my colleagues at other schools, I do feel that mission was accomplished.

NOTES

Introduction . . . to the Undead

1. Bishop 2008; Dendle 2007.

2. Brooks 2003; Louison 2009; Ma 2010.

3. Bolger 2010.

4. For prestigious fiction, see Whitehead 2011. For the revisionist pre-Victorian literature, see Austen and Grahame-Smith 2009; the success of *Pride and Prejudice and Zombies* has spawned a number of similarly reinterpreted classics ranging from children's stories (Baum and Thomas 2009; Carroll and Cook 2009), to touchstones in American literature (Twain and Czolgosz 2009), to the history of the Beatles (Goldsher 2010).

5. Katy Harshberger of St. Martin's Press, quoted in Wilson 2009.

6. Bishop 2008; Newitz, 2008; VanDusky 2008.

7. Koblentz 2010; Stern 2002–3.

8. Dendle 2007, 54.

9. Buus 2009; Grayson, Davies, and Philpott 2009.

10. See, for example, University of Florida, *Zombie Attack: Disaster Preparedness Simulation Exercise #5*, http://www.astro.ufl.edu/~jybarra/zombieplan.pdf (accessed July 15, 2010).

11. Wexler 2008. See also Humans vs Zombies, "About HVZ," http://humansvszombies.org/About (accessed July 15, 2010).

12. John B. Snow, "Surviving the Undead: Zombie Guns," *Outdoor Life*, March 3, 2010, http://www.outdoorlife.com/photos/gallery/survival/2010/03/surviving-undead-zombie-guns (accessed July 15, 2010).

13. Carlson 2003; Chyba and Greniger 2004; Klotz and Sylvester 2009; Koblentz 2010; Stern 2002–3.

14. Berlinski 2009; Davis 1988.

15. US Strategic Command 2011.

16. Martin Dempsey, quoted in Barnes 2014.

17. Twitchell 1985, 273.

18. Waldmann 2009.

19. Significant exceptions include Brooks 2006 and Grant 2010.

20. Cooke 2009, chap. 7. Obvious and important exceptions are Joss Whedon's TV series *Buffy the Vampire Slayer* (1997–2003) and *Angel* (1999–2004).

21. On teen vampires in books, see L. J. Smith's Vampire Diaries series (1991–); Charlaine Harris's Southern Vampire Mysteries (aka the True Blood series, 2001–); Stephenie Meyer's Twilight series (2005–); Richelle Mead's Vampire Academy series (2006–); D. C. Cast and Kristin Cast's House of Night series (2007–); and Melissa De La Cruz's Blue Bloods series (2007–); and that's just for starters.

22. Grayson, Davies, and Philpott 2009, 157; emphasis in the original.

The Zombie Literature

1. Bishop 2009; Christie and Lauro 2011; Harper 2002; Loudermilk 2003.

2. Chalmers 1996; Dennett 1995; Moody 1994.

3. Foster, Ratneiks, and Raybould 2000; Hughes et al. 2009; Hughes, Wappler, and Labandeira 2010.

4. Rudolf and Antonovics 2007.

5. Schlozman 2011 Vass 2001.

6. Cassi 2009.

7. Cooke, Jahanian, and McPherson 2005.

8. Smith? et al. 2009, 146.

9. See Gelman 2010; Messer 2010; and Rossman 2010.

10. Nicolaides, Cueto-Felgueroso, and Juanes 2013.

11. The full list is available at http://zombieresearch.org/advisoryboard.html (accessed July 15, 2010).

12. See, for example, Quiggin 2010.

13. On the economic research into vampires, see Hartl and Mehlmann 1982; Hartl, Mehlmann, and Novak 1992; and Snower 1982. For the nascent economics literature on zombies, see Whitman and Dow 2014.

14. Thomas Hobbes, *Leviathan*, part 1, chap. 13, para. 9; Kautilya, *The Arthashastra*, book 4, chap. 3, para. 13–15; Sun Tzu, *Art of War*, chap. 11, line 14; Thucydides, *History of the Peloponnesian War*, book 2, para. 50.

15. On UFOs, see Wendt and Duvall 2008. On wizards and international relations, see Nexon and Neumann 2006; on hobbits and international relations, see Ruane and James 2008. Regarding Cylons in the Battlestar Galactica series, see Buzan 2010 and Kiersey and Neumann 2013. Buus 2009, Davies 2010, and Molloy 2003, discuss vampires and international studies. Dixit 2012 tackles *Doctor Who*. For recent political science work on zombies, see Blanton 2013; Coker 2013; Hall 2011; and Youde 2012.

16. Goldsmith 2007; Hoyt and Brooks 2003–4; Klotz and Sylvester 2009.

17. Suskind 2006.

18. Stern 2002–3.

19. Clarke 1999; Cordesman 2001.

20. Drezner 2009; US Strategic Command 2011.

21. Sparks, Nelson, and Campbell 1997.

22. Markovsky and Thye 2001.

23. Crawford 2000; Gray and Ropeik 2002; Moïsi 2007; Strong 1990.

24. Maberry 2008, 267.

25. Ibid. See also Bishop 2009.

26. King, Keohane, and Verba 1994, 29–30.

27. Ferguson 2004; Haass 2008; Naim 2013; Schweller 2010.

28. See Der Derian 2002, and US Strategic Command 2011, 20. In 2010 Max Brooks addressed cadets at the US Naval War College at the behest of the school commandant. See Max Brooks, "The Naval War College," http://max brooks.com/news/2010/04/12/the-us-naval-war-college/ (accessed July 15, 2010).

29. On simulations, see Van Belle 1998; on agent-based modeling, see Cederman 2003.

30. See Buus 2009; ; Buzan 2010; Cordesman 2001; Hulsman and Mitchell 2009; Kiersey and Neumann 2013; Muller 2008; Van Belle, Mash, and Braunwarth 2010; Weber 2006; and Weldes 2003.

31. Solnit 2009, 120–34.

32. Tetlock 2005.

33. Jackson and Nexon 2009; Lake 2011.

34. Frieden, Lake, and Schultz 2009; Lake 2011.

Defining a Zombie

1. US Strategic Command 2011, 5–6.

2. See also Brooks 2003, 1.

3. There are exceptions. In Dominic Mitchell's *In the Flesh*, the idea that a zombie bite turns one into a zombie is dismissed as an urban legend.

4. This definition also excludes some more recent characters with quasi-zombie properties, like the Reavers in Joss Whedon's TV series *Firefly* (2002) or the Virals in Cronin 2010.

Distracting Debates about Flesh-Eating Ghouls

1. For recent examples of the variegated approaches to the undead, see Adams 2008 and Golden 2010.

2. See Keene 2004 and 2005, as well as Wellington 2006a, 2006b, and 2007.

3. King 2006.

4. Brooks 2003, 2006.

5. Recht 2006.

6. Cordesman 2001; Koblentz 2010.

7. Perrow 1984.

8. Klotz and Sylvester 2009.

9. Dendle 2001, 121; Twohy 2008, 16.

10. Bishop 2009, 21; Maberry 2008, 22–23.

11. For a recent and concise summary of this debate, see Levin 2004.

12. Ma 2010, 2–3.

13. Brooks 2003, 13–14.

14. Maberry 2008, chap. 3.

15. The most prominent outlier is Zack Snyder's 2004 remake of *Dawn of the Dead*, in which the infection was slow but the zombies were fast.

16. Cordesman 2001, 11; Maberry 2008, 172.

17. US Strategic Command 2011, 16.

The *Realpolitik* of the Living Dead

1. Space constraints prevent a further exploration of the myriad intraparadigmatic divisions of realism. For classical realism, see Morgenthau 1948. For neoclassical realism, see Rose 1998 and Zakaria 1998. On postclassical realism, see Brooks 1997. Mearsheimer 2001 provides the exemplar of offensive realism. For a good example of defensive realism, see Snyder 1991. For a critique, see Legro and Moravcsik 1999.

2. Walt 1987.

3. Waltz 1979, 105.

4. Grieco 1988; see also Powell 1991 and Snidal 1991.

5. Herz 1950; Jervis 1978.

6. Mearsheimer 2001.

7. Mearsheimer and Walt 2007; Walt 2005.

8. Waltz 1979, 76–77.

9. Gilpin 1981; Kennedy 1987; Kim 1992; Organski 1958.

10. Diamond 1999; McNeill 1976; Price-Smith 2002.

11. Anbarci, Escaleras, and Register 2005; Brancati 2007; Cohen and Werker 2008; Kahn 2005; Nel and Richarts 2008.

12. US Strategic Command 2011, 23.

13. Glaser and Kaufmann 1998.

14. Brooks 2006, 105–11.

15. On containment, see Gaddis 1982 and Kennan 1984.

16. Christensen and Snyder 1990; Mearsheimer 2001.
17. Mastanduno 1992.
18. Hughes 2007.
19. Brancati 2007; Nel and Righarts 2008.
20. Walt 1996.
21. Mearsheimer 2001, 152–55.

Regulating the Undead in a Liberal World Order

1. Space constraints prevent an extended discussion of the different varieties of the liberal paradigm. On Kantian liberalism, see Doyle 1983; on commercial liberalism, see Russett and Oneal 1997. Keohane 1984 provides the best development of neoliberal institutionalism, and Moravcsik 1997 develops ideational liberalism. On democratic liberalism, see Doyle 1986, and on liberal internationalism, see Ikenberry 2000.

2. Hardin 1982; Olson 1971.
3. Axelrod 1984; Axelrod and Keohane 1985.
4. Keohane and Nye 1978; Lipson 1984.
5. Drezner 2000; Keohane 1984; Martin 1992.
6. Martin 2000; Simmons 2009.
7. Powell 1991; Snidal 1991.
8. Kimball 2006; Knobler, Mahmoud, and Lemon 2006; Koblentz 2010, 102–3.

9. Harper 2002; Lauro and Embry 2008; Webb and Byrnard 2008.

10. Axelrod 1984; Fudenberg and Maskin 1986.
11. Khan 2011.

12. Raustiala and Victor 2004. US Strategic Command notes that an array of international treaties and agreements, including the United Nations Charter, were consulted in the preparation of their counterzombie plan. See US Strategic Command 2011, 7–8.

13. Drezner 2007.
14. Brooks 2006, 264–69.
15. Ikenberry 2000, 2010.

16. Chayes and Chayes 1993; Downs, Rocke, and Barsoom 1994.

17. Haftendorn, Keohane, and Wallander 1999; Lake 2001.

18. Hoyt and Brooks 2003–4.

19. Brooks 2006, Grant 2010.

20. Marlin-Bennett, Wilson, and Walton 2010.

21. Barrett 2007b; Nadelmann 1990.

22. Barrett 2007a.

23. Flores and Smith 2010; Kahn 2005.

24. Kahn 2005; Ó Gráda 2009; Sen 1983.

25. Fidler 2004.

26. Brooks 2006, 47.

27. Drezner 2007; Keck and Sikkink 1998; Sell 2003.

28. The Citizens for Undead Rights and Equality manifesto—which calls for equal rights and a raising of the mandatory retirement age to be higher than "dead," can be found at http://www.votecure.com/vote/?p=13 (accessed July 15, 2010).

29. Fidler 2009.

30. Carpenter 2007.

The Social Construction of Zombies

1. For a state-centric approach, see Wendt 1999; for a more non-state-centric take, see Holzscheiter 2005. Der Derian and Shapiro 1989 provide a more interpretivist approach.

2. Tannenwald 1999, 2005.

3. Johnston 2001.

4. Mercer 1995.

5. Mitzen 2006.

6. Cooke 2009, chap. 7; Russell 2005.

7. Webb and Byrnard 2008, 86; emphasis added.

8. Wendt and Duvall 2008.

9. Wendt 1992.

10. Price-Smith 2003; Strong 1990.

11. Adler and Barnett 1998.

12. Durodié and Wessely 2002; Furedi 2007; Glass and Schoch-Spana 2001; Quarantelli 2004; Tierney 2004.

13. Solnit 2009, 2.

14. Snyder 2002. Even under circumstances of famine, however, Ó Gráda (2009) finds minimal evidence of cannibalism, for example.

15. Mercer 1995.

16. Wendt 2003.

17. Furedi 2007, 487.

18. Clarke 2002; Grayson, Davies, and Philpott 2008; Mitchell et al. 2000; Tierney, Bevc, and Kuligowski 2006.

19. Webb and Byrnard 2008, 84.

20. Finnemore and Sikkink 1998.

21. Brooks 2006, 157–58.

22. Nye 2004.

The Supergendered Politics of the Posthuman World

1. Sylvester 2013.

2. Dietz 2003, 400.

3. Murphy 1996; Peterson 1992; Sylvester 2002; Tickner 1992; Tickner and Sjoberg 2013.

4. Unfortunately, this marginalization extends to women scholars themselves. See Maliniak, Powers, and Walter 2013.

5. Tickner 1992.

6. Chin 1998; Enloe 1989, 2013; Sjoberg and Gentry 2007.

7. Cox 1981. See also the exchange between Tickner 1997 and Keohane 1998 for more on this schism.

8. See, for example, Zalewski and Runyan 2013.

9. Caprioli 2003, 2005; Caprioli and Boyer 2001.

10. Buck, Gallant, and Nossal 1998.

11. Steans 1998, 5.

12. Moon 1997.

13. Tickner 1992, 41.

14. Chowdhry and Nair 2002; Crenshaw 1989; Sylvester 2002.

15. Marion 2011, 42 and 127.

A Very Important Note about Zombie Networks

1. See Hafner-Burton, Kahler, and Montgomery 2009; Hafner-Burton and Montgomery 2006; Kahler 2009; Lazer 2011; Oatley et al. 2013; Slaughter 2009; and Ward, Stovel, and Sacks 2011.

2. Carpenter 2007a, 2007b, 2011.

Neoconservatism and the Axis of Evil Dead

1. For scholarly assessments of neoconservatism as a theoretical paradigm, see Caverley 2010; Fukuyama 2006; Rapport 2008; and Williams 2005.

2. Fukuyama 1992.

3. Bolton 2007; Krauthammer 2004.

4. Bolton 2007; Kagan 2008.

5. Caverley 2010, 602–7; Kagan and Kagan 2000; Kristol and Kagan 1996. On classical realist skepticism about the ability of democracies to practice foreign policy, see Kennan 1984.

6. Bolton 2007; Frum and Perle 2004; Kagan 2008; Kristol and Kagan 2000; Podhoretz 2007.

7. Kagan 2003.

8. Boot 2006; Fukuyama 2006; Kagan 2003.

9. On the neoconservative faith in the ability of the United States to create its own reality, see Suskind 2004.

10. Kagan and Kagan 2000; Kristol 1983; Kristol and Brooks 1997; Kristol and Kagan 1996.

11. Smith? et al. 2009.

12. Frum and Perle 2004.

13. US Strategic Command 2011, 4.

14. Podhoretz 2007.

15. Brooks 2006, 104; emphasis in the original.

Domestic Politics: Are All Zombie Politics Local?

1. See Bueno de Mesquita et al. 2003; Milner 1997; Putnam 1988; Weeks 2008.

2. Risse-Kappen 1991.

3. Krasner 1978.

4. Jakobson and Knox 2010.

5. Kaufmann 2004; Ornstein and Mann 2006.

6. Howell and Pevehouse 2007.

7. Baum 2002.

8. Eichenberg 2005; Feaver and Gelpi 2004.

9. Voters reward politicians more for postdisaster performance more than preventive measures. See Healy and Malhorta 2009.

10. Burbach 1994; Kohut and Stokes 2006.

11. Pew Research Center 2009 and 2013.

12. US Strategic Command 2011, 14.

13. Przeworski and Wallerstein 1988.

14. Stanger 2009.

15. This result is consistent with Milner 1997.

16. Jakobson and Knox 2010.

17. Li 2009.

18. Acemoglu and Robinson 2012; Bueno de Mesquita et al. 2003.

19. Wallace 2011.

20. Evans, Jacobsen, and Putnam 1993; Putnam 1988.

Bureaucratic Politics: The "Pulling and Hauling" of Zombies

1. Barnett and Finnemore 2004.

2. Wilson 1989.

3. Allison 1971; Halperin 1974.

4. Cohen, March, and Olsen 1972.

5. On legislative constraints, see Weingast and Moran 1983; for executive branch constraints, see Moe 1990; for an integrative approach, see Hammond and Knott 1996.

6. Simon 1976.

7. Zegart 2007.

8. Cordesman 2001.

9. Keene 2005, 123.

10. Solnit 2009, 125.

11. Brooks 2006, 94–100.

12. Brooks 2003, 155.

13. The air force loses most of its combat capabilities in favor of transport and logistics.

14. Brooks 2006, 145.

15. Hafner-Burton, Kahler, and Montgomery 2009; Slaughter 2004.

We're Only Human: Psychological Responses to the Undead

1. Whitehead 2011, 137.

2. Stern 2002–3.

3. Mori 1970.

4. Price-Smith 2002; Strong 1990, 252–54.

5. Bynam and Pollack 2001; Waltz 1959.

6. Jervis 1976.

7. Houghton 1996; Khong 1992; Neustadt and May 1986.

8. Maberry 2008, 39.

9. Brooks 2003, 154.

10. Mercer 1996.

11. Kahneman and Tversky 1979; Levy 1997.

12. Jervis 1992.

13. Kahneman and Renshon 2007.

14. Weinstein 1980.

15. Glass and Schoch-Spana 2001.

16. Thaler and Sunstein 2008.

17. Brooks 2003.

18. Janis 1972.

19. Sunstein and Vermeule 2008.

Conclusion . . . or So You Think

1. Paris 2001.
2. Goldstein 2011; Mueller 2009b; Pinker 2011.
3. Most and Starr 1984.
4. Berlin 1996; Katzenstein and Okawara 2001–2; Sil and Katzenstein 2010.
5. Hirschman 1970, 341.

Epilogue: Bringing the Brain Back In

1. For a complete reading of *Z Is for Zombie*, see Woerner 2012.
2. Phillips 2014.
3. Stern 2002–3.
4. See, for example, Collins 2012a, 2012b, 2013; Krugman 2013; Wilentz 2012.
5. See REI, "13 Essential Tools for Surviving a Zombie Outbreak," http://www.rei.com/features/infographics/zombie.html?stop_mobi=yes (accessed April 4, 2014); and Zombie Safe House Competition, http://zombiesafehouse .wordpress.com/(accessed April 4, 2014).
6. Khan 2011.
7. See US Centers for Disease Control and Prevention, "Preparedness 101: Zombie Pandemic," http://www.cdc.gov /phpr/zombies/#/page/1 (accessed April 4, 2014).
8. US Strategic Command 2011, 1–2.
9. US Strategic Command 2011, 2.
10. Campbell 2012.
11. Houghton 1996; Khong 1992; Snidal 1985.
12. LaPierre 2013; emphasis in the original.
13. See, for example, Waters et al. 2013, Wilson 2014, and Yglesias 2014.
14. Collins 2013.
15. Deslatte 2014.
16. On the secular trends toward less violence and carnage, see Goldstein 2011; Mueller 2009b; and Pinker 2011. On reduced threat expectations in the United States, see Zenko and Cohen 2012.

REFERENCES

Acemoglu, Daron, and James A. Robinson. 2012. *Why Nations Fail: The Origins of Power, Prosperity, and Poverty*. New York: Crown Business.

Adams, John Joseph, ed. 2008. *The Living Dead*. San Francisco: Night Shade Books.

Adler, Emanuel, and Michael Barnett, eds. 1998. *Security Communities*. Cambridge: Cambridge University Press.

Allison, Graham. 1971. *Essence of Decision: Explaining the Cuban Missile Crisis*. Boston: Little, Brown.

Aquilina, Carmelo, and Julian Hughes. 2006. "The Return of the Living Dead: Agency Lost and Found?" In *Dementia: Mind, Meaning and the Person*, ed. Julian Hughes, Stephen Louw, and Steven Sabat, 143–62. New York: Oxford University Press.

Austen, Jane, and Seth Grahame-Smith. 2009. *Pride and Prejudice and Zombies*. Philadelphia: Quirk Books.

Axelrod, Robert. 1984. *The Evolution of Cooperation*. New York: Basic Books.

Axelrod, Robert, and Robert Keohane. 1985. "Achieving Cooperation under Anarchy: Strategies and Institutions." *World Politics* 38 (October): 226–54.

Barnes, Julian E. 2014, April 1. "Gen. Dempsey Finds Military Lessons in Literature and a Zombie Attack." *Wall Street Journal*, http://blogs.wsj.com/washwire/2014/04/01/gen-dempsey-finds-military-lessons-in-literature-and-a-zombie-attack/. Accessed April 23, 2014.

Barnett, Michael, and Martha Finnemore. 2004. *Rules for the World: International Organizations in Global Politics*. Ithaca, NY: Cornell University Press.

Barrett, Scott. 2007a. "The Smallpox Eradication Game." *Public Choice* 130 (January): 179–207.

———. 2007b. *Why Cooperate? The Incentive to Supply Global Public Goods*. New York: Oxford University Press.

Baum, L. Frank, and Ryan Thomas. 2009. *The Undead World of Oz*. Winnipeg, Manitoba, Canada: Coscom.

Baum, Matthew. 2002. "The Constituent Foundations of the Rally-round-the-Flag Phenomenon." *International Studies Quarterly* 46 (June): 263–98.

Berlin, Isaiah. 1996, October 3. "On Political Judgment." *New York Review of Books*, 26–30.

Berlinski, Mischa. 2009, September. "Into the Zombie Underworld." *Men's Journal*, http://www.mensjournal.com/into-the-zombie-underworld. Accessed July 15, 2010.

Bishop, Kyle. 2008. "The Sub-Subaltern Monster: Imperialist Hegemony and the Cinematic Voodoo Zombie." *Journal of American Culture* 31 (June): 141–52.

———. 2009. "Dead Man Still Walking: Explaining the Zombie Renaissance." *Journal of Popular Film and Television* 37 (Spring): 16–25.

Blanton, Robert G. 2013. "Zombies and International Relations: A Simple Guide for Bringing the Undead into Your Classroom." *International Studies Perspectives* 14 (January): 1–13.

Bolger, Kevin. 2010. *Zombiekins*. New York: Razorbill.

Bolton, John. 2007. *Surrender Is Not an Option*. New York: Threshold.

Boot, Max. 2006. *War Made New: Technology, Warfare, and the Course of History, 1500 to Today*. New York: Gotham.

Brancati, Dawn. 2007. "Political Aftershocks: The Impact of Earthquakes on Intrastate Conflict." *Journal of Conflict Resolution* 51 (October): 715–43.

Brooks, Max. 2003. *The Zombie Survival Guide: Complete Protection from the Living Dead*. New York: Three Rivers.

———. 2006. *World War Z: An Oral History of the Zombie War*. New York: Three Rivers.

Brooks, Stephen. 1997. "Dueling Realisms." *International Organization* 51 (July): 445–77.

Buck, Lori, Nicole Gallant, and Kim Richard Nossal. 1998. "Sanctions as a Gendered Instrument of Statecraft: The Case of Iraq." *Review of International Studies* 24 (January): 69–84.

Bueno de Mesquita, Bruce, James Morrow, Randolph Siverson, and Alistair Smith. 2003. *The Logic of Political Survival*. Cambridge, MA: MIT Press.

Burbach, David. 1994. *Presidential Approval and the Use of Force*. Working Paper, Defense and Arms Control Studies Program, Massachusetts Institute of Technology.

Buus, Stephanie. 2009. "Hell on Earth: Threats, Citizens and the State from Buffy to Beck." *Cooperation and Conflict* 44 (December): 400–419.

Buzan, Barry. 2010. "America in Space: The International Relations of *Star Trek* and *Battlestar Galactica*." *Millennium* 39 (January): 175–80.

Bynam, Daniel, and Kenneth Pollack. 2001. "Let Us Now Praise Great Men: Bringing the Statesman Back In." *International Security* 25 (Spring): 107–46.

Campbell, Andy. 2012, June 1. "CDC Denies Existence of Zombies Despite Cannibal Incidents." *Huffington Post*, http://www.huffingtonpost.com/2012/06/01/cdc-denies-zombies-existence_n_1562141.html. Accessed April 4, 2014.

Caprioli, Mary. 2003. "Gender Equality and State Aggression: The Impact of Domestic Gender Equality on State First Use of Force." *International Interactions* 29 (Summer): 195–214.

———. 2005. "Primed for Violence: The Role of Gender Inequality in Predicting Internal Conflict." *International Studies Quarterly* 49 (Spring): 161–78.

Caprioli, Mary, and Mark A. Boyer. 2001. "Gender, Violence, and International Crisis." *Journal of Conflict Resolution* 45 (December): 503–18.

Carlson, Robert. 2003. "The Pace and Proliferation of Biological Technologies." *Biosecurity and Bioterrorism* 1 (September): 203–14.

Carpenter, Charli. 2007a. "Setting the Advocacy Agenda: Issues and Non-Issues around Children and Armed Conflict." *International Studies Quarterly* 51 (March): 99–120.

———. 2007b. "Studying Issue (Non)-Adoption in Transnational Advocacy Networks." *International Organization* 61 (Summer): 643–67.

————. 2011. "Vetting the Advocacy Agenda: Network Centrality and the Paradox of Weapons Norms." *International Organization* 66 (January): 69–102.

Carroll, Lewis, and Nickolas Cook. 2009. *Alice in Zombieland*. Winnipeg, Manitoba, Canada: Coscom.

Cassi, Davide. 2009. "Target Annihilation by Diffusing Particles in Inhomogenous Geometries." *Physical Review E* 80 (September): 1–3.

Caverley, Jonathan. 2010. "Power and Democratic Weakness: Neoconservatism and Neoclassical Realism." *Millennium* 38 (May): 593–614.

Cederman, Lars-Erik. 2003. "Modeling the Size of Wars: From Billiard Balls to Sandpiles." *American Political Science Review* 97 (February): 135–50.

Chalmers, David. 1996. *The Conscious Mind: In Search of a Fundamental Theory*. New York: Oxford University Press.

Chayes, Abram, and Antonia Handler Chayes. 1993. "On Compliance." *International Organization* 47 (Spring): 175–206.

Chin, Christine. 1998. *In Service and Servitude: Foreign Female Domestic Workers and the Malaysian "Modernity" Project*. New York: Columbia University Press.

Chowdhry, Geeta, and Sheila Nair, eds. 2002. *Power, Postcolonialism and International Relations: Reading Race, Gender and Class*. London: Routledge.

Christensen, Thomas, and Jack Snyder. 1990. "Chain Gangs and Passed Bucks: Predicting Alliance Patterns under Multipolarity." *International Organization* 44 (March): 137–68.

Christie, Deborah, and Sara Juliet Lauro, eds. 2011. *Better Off Dead: The Evolution of the Zombie as Post-Human*. New York: Fordham University Press.

Chyba, Christopher, and Alex Greniger. 2004. "Biotechnology and Bioterrorism: An Unprecedented World." *Survival* 46 (January): 143–62.

Clarke, Lee. 1999. *Mission Improbable: Using Fantasy Documents to Tame Disaster*. Chicago: University of Chicago Press.

————. 2002. "Panic: Myth or Reality?" *Contexts* 1 (Fall): 21–26.

Cohen, Charles, and Eric Werker. 2008. "The Political Economy of 'Natural' Disasters." *Journal of Conflict Resolution* 52 (December): 795–819.

Cohen, Michael, James March, and Johan Olsen. 1972. "A Garbage Can Model of Organizational Choice." *Administrative Science Quarterly* 17 (March): 1–25.

Coker, Christopher. 2013. "Dying to Fight: Some Reflections on Zombies and War." *International Politics Reviews* 1 (December): 91–99.

Collins, Gail. 2012a, October 5. "Of Hooters, Zombies and Senators." *New York Times*.

———. 2012b, December 12. "Another Boom Year." *New York Times*.

———. 2013, March 8. "Senators Bearing Arms." *New York Times*.

Comaroff, Jean, and John Comaroff. 2002. "Alien-Nation: Zombies, Immigrants, and Millenial Capitalism." *South Atlantic Quarterly* 101 (Fall): 779–805.

Cooke, Evan, Farnam Jahanian, and Danny McPherson. 2005. "The Zombie Roundup: Understanding, Detecting, and Disturbing Botnets." In *Proceedings of the First Workshop on Steps to Reducing Unwanted Traffic on the Internet (STRUTI)*, 39–44. Cambridge, MA: Steps to Reducing Unwanted Traffic on the Internet.

Cooke, Jennifer. 2009. *Legacies of Plague in Literature, Theory and Film*. New York: Palgrave Macmillan.

Cordesman, Anthony. 2001, September 29. "Biological Warfare and the 'Buffy Paradigm.'" Washington, DC: Center for Strategic and International Studies.

Cox, Robert. 1981. "Social Forces, States and World Orders: Beyond International Relations Theory." *Millennium* 10 (Spring): 126–55.

Crawford, Neta. 2000. "The Passion of World Politics: Propositions on Emotion and Emotional Relationships." *International Security* 24 (Spring): 116–56.

Crenshaw, Kimberle. 1989. "Demarginalizing the Intersection of Race and Sex: A Black Feminist Critique of Antidiscrimination Doctrine, Feminist Theory, and Antiracist Politics." *University of Chicago Legal Forum* 140: 139–67.

Cronin, Justin. 2010. *The Passage*. New York: Ballantine.

Davies, Matt. 2010. "'You Can't Charge Innocent People for Saving Their Lives!' Work in Buffy the Vampire Slayer." *International Political Sociology* 4 (June): 178–95.

Davis, Wade. 1985. *The Serpent and the Rainbow*. New York: Simon and Schuster.

———. 1988. *Passage of Darkness: The Ethnobiology of the Haitian Zombie*. Chapel Hill: University of North Carolina Press.

Dendle, Peter. 2001. *The Zombie Movie Encyclopedia*. Los Angeles: McFarland.

———. 2007. "The Zombie as Barometer of Cultural Anxiety." In *Monsters and the Monstrous: Myths and Metaphors of Enduring Evil*, ed. Niall Scott, 45–57. New York: Rodopi.

Dennett, Daniel. 1995. "The Unimagined Preposterousness of Zombies." *Journal of Consciousness Studies* 2 (April): 322–25.

Der Derian, James. 2002. "9/11: Before, After, and In Between." In *Understanding September 11*, ed. Craig Calhoun, Paul Price, and Ashley Timmer, 146–59. New York: New Press.

Der Derian, James, and Michael Shapiro, eds. 1989. *International/Intertextual Relations: Postmodern Readings of World Politics*. Lexington, MA: Lexington.

Deslatte, Aaron. 2014. "'Zombie Apocalypse' in the Florida Senate?" *Orlando Sentinel*, April 30. http://www.orlandosen tinel.com/news/blogs/political-pulse/os-zombie-apoca lypse-in-the-florida-senate-20140430,0,2409227.post.

Diamond, Jared. 1999. *Guns, Germs, and Steel: The Fates of Human Societies*. New York: W. W. Norton.

Dietz, Mary G. 2003. "Current Controversies in Feminist Theory." *Annual Review of Political Science* 6: 399–431.

Dixit, Priya. 2012. "Relating to Difference: Aliens and Alienness in *Doctor Who* and International Relations." *International Studies Perspectives* 13 (July): 289–306.

Downs, George, David Rocke, and Peter Barsoom. 1994. "Is the Good News about Compliance Good News about Cooperation?" *International Organization* 50 (Summer): 379–406.

Doyle, Michael. 1983. "Kant, Liberal Legacies, and Foreign Affairs." *Philosophy and Public Affairs* 12 (Summer): 205–35.

———. 1986. "Liberalism and World Politics." *American Political Science Review* 80 (December): 1151–69.

Drezner, Daniel W. 2000. "Bargaining, Enforcement, and Multilateral Economic Sanctions: When Is Cooperation Counterproductive?" *International Organization* 54 (Winter): 73–102.

———. 2007. *All Politics Is Global: Explaining International Regulatory Regimes*. Princeton, NJ: Princeton University Press.

———. 2008. "The Realist Tradition in American Public Opinion." *Perspectives on Politics* 6 (March): 51–70.

———, ed. 2009. *Avoiding Trivia: The Role of Strategic Planning in American Foreign Policy*. Washington, DC: Brookings Institution Press.

Durodié, Bill, and Simon Wessely. 2002. "Resilience or Panic? The Public and Terrorist Attack." *Lancet* 360 (December 14): 1901–2.

Efthimiou, Costas, and Sohang Gandhi. 2007. "Cinema Fiction vs. Physics Reality: Ghosts, Vampires, and Zombies." *Skeptical Inquirer* 31 (July–August): 27–38.

Eichenberg, Richard. 2005. "Victory Has Many Friends: U.S. Public Opinion and the Use of Force, 1981–2005," *International Security* 30 (Summer): 140–77.

Enloe, Cynthia H. 1989. *Bananas, Beaches and Bases: Making Feminist Sense of International Politics*. Berkeley and Los Angeles: University of California Press.

———. 2013. *Seriously! Investigating Crashes and Crises as if Women Mattered*. Berkeley and Los Angeles: University of California Press.

Evans, Peter, Harold Jacobson, and Robert Putnam, eds. 1993. *Double-Edged Diplomacy: International Bargaining and Domestic Politics*. Berkeley and Los Angeles: University of California Press.

Fay, Jennifer. 2008. "Dead Subjectivity: *White Zombie*, Black Baghdad." *CR: The New Centennial Review* 8 (Spring): 81–101.

Feaver, Peter, and Chrisopher Gelpi. 2004. *Choosing Your Battles*. Princeton, NJ: Princeton University Press.

Ferguson, Niall. 2004. "A World without Power," *Foreign Policy* (July–August): 32–39.

Fidler, David. 2004. *SARS: Governance and the Globalization of Disease*. New York: Palgrave Macmillan.

———. 2009. "H1N1 after Action Review: Learning from the Unexpected, the Success and the Fear." *Future Microbiology* 4 (September): 767–69.

Finnemore, Martha, and Kathryn Sikkink. 1998. "International Norm Dynamics and Political Change." *International Organization* 52 (October): 887–917.

Flores, Alejandro Quiroz, and Alistair Smith. 2010. "Surviving Disasters." Paper presented at the annual meeting of the International Political Economy Society, Cambridge, MA.

Foster, Kevin, Francis Ratnieks, and Alan Raybould. 2000. "Do Hornets Have Zombie Workers?" *Molecular Ecology* 9 (June): 735–42.

Frieden, Jeffry A., David A. Lake, and Kenneth A. Schultz. 2008. *World Politics: Interests, Interactions, Institutions*. New York: W. W. Norton.

Frum, David, and Richard Perle. 2004. *An End to Evil: How to Win the War on Terror*. New York: Random House.

Fudenberg, Drew, and Eric Maskin. 1986. "The Folk Theorem in Repeated Games with Discounting or with Incomplete Information." *Econometrica* 54 (May): 533–54.

Fukuyama, Francis. 1992. *The End of History and the Last Man*. New York: Free Press.

———. 2006. *America at the Crossroads*. New Haven, CT: Yale University Press.

Furedi, Frank. 2007. "The Changing Meaning of Disaster." *Area* 39 (December): 482–89.

Gaddis, John Lewis. 1982. *Strategies of Containment*. New York: Oxford University Press.

Gelman, Andrew. 2010. "*How Many Zombies Do You Know?*" *Using Indirect Survey Methods to Measure Alien Attacks and*

Outbreaks of the Undead. Working paper, Department of Statistics, Columbia University.

Gilpin, Robert. 1981. *War and Change in World Politics.* New York: Cambridge University Press.

Glaser, Charles, and Chaim Kaufmann. 1998. "What is the Offense-Defense Balance and How Can We Measure It?" *International Security* 22 (Spring): 44–82.

Glass, Thomas, and Monica Schoch-Spana. 2001. "Bioterrorism and the People: How to Vaccinate a City against Panic." *Clinical Infectious Diseases* 34 (December): 217–23.

Golden, Christopher, ed. 2010. *The New Dead: A Zombie Anthology.* New York: St. Martin's.

Goldsher, Alan. 2010. *Paul Is Undead: The British Zombie Invasion.* New York: Gallery Books.

Goldsmith, Jack. 2007. *The Terror Presidency: Law and Judgment inside the Bush Administration.* New York: W. W. Norton.

Goldstein, Joshua S. 2011. *Winning the War on War: The Decline of Armed Conflict Worldwide.* New York: Penguin.

Grant, Mira. 2010. *Feed.* New York: Orbit.

Gray, George, and David Ropeik. 2002. "Dealing with the Dangers of Fear: The Role of Risk Communication." *Health Affairs* 6 (November–December): 106–16.

Grayson, Kyle, Matt Davies, and Simon Philpott. 2009. "Pop Goes IR? Researching the Popular Culture–World Politics Continuum." *Politics* 29 (October): 155–63.

Grieco, Joseph. 1988. "Anarchy and the Limits of Cooperation." *International Organization* 42 (June): 485–507.

Haass, Richard. 2008. "The Age of Nonpolarity." *Foreign Affairs* 87 (May–June): 44–56.

Hafner-Burton, Emilie M., Miles Kahler, and Alexander H. Montgomery. 2009. "Network Analysis for International Relations," *International Organization* 63 (July): 559–92.

Hafner-Burton, Emilie M., and Alexander H. Montgomery. 2006. "Power Positions: International Organizations, Social Networks, and Conflict." *Journal of Conflict Resolution* 50 (January): 3–27.

Haftendorn, Helga, Robert Keohane, and Celeste Wallander, eds. 1999. *Imperfect Unions: Security Institutions over Time and Space*. New York: Oxford University Press.

Hall, Derek. 2011. "Varieties of Zombieism: Approaching Comparative Political Economy through *28 Days Later* and *Wild Zero*." *International Studies Perspectives* 12 (January): 1–17.

Halperin, Morton. 1974. *Bureaucratic Politics and Foreign Policy*. Washington, DC: Brookings Institution Press.

Hammond, Thomas, and Jack Knott. 1996. "Who Controls the Bureaucracy?" *Journal of Law, Economics, and Organization* 12 (April): 119–66.

Hardin, Russell. 1982. *Collective Action*. Washington: Resources for the Future.

Harper, Stephen. 2002. "Zombies, Malls, and the Consumerism Debate." *Americana* 1 (Fall): article 4.

Hartl, Richard, and Alexander Mehlmann. 1982. "The Transylvanian Problem of Renewable Resources." *Recherche opérationelle/Operations Research* 16 (November): 379–90.

Hartl, Richard, Alexander Mehlmann, and Andreas Novak. 1992. "Cycles of Fear: Periodic Bloodsucking Rates for Vampires." *Journal of Optimization Theory and Applications* 75 (December): 559–68.

Healy, Andrew, and Neil Malhorta. 2009. "Myopic Voters and Natural Disaster Policy." *American Political Science Review* 103 (August): 387–406.

Hendrix, Grady. 2007, May 10. "Mocha Zombies." *Slate*, http://www.slate.com/id/2165990. Accessed July 15, 2010.

Herz, John. 1950. "Idealist Internationalism and the Security Dilemma." *World Politics* 2 (January): 157–80.

Hirschman, Albert. 1970. "The Search for Paradigms as a Hindrance to Understanding." *World Politics* 22 (April): 329–43.

Holzscheiter, Anna. 2005. "Discourse as Capability: Non-State Actors' Capital in Global Governance." *Millennium: Journal of International Studies* 33 (June): 723–46.

Houghton, David Patrick. 1996. "The Role of Analogical Reasoning in Novel Foreign-Policy Situations," *British Journal of Political Science* 26 (October): 523–52.

Howell, Will, and Jon Pevehouse. 2007. *While Dangers Gather: Congressional Checks on Presidential War Powers*. Princeton, NJ: Princeton University Press.

Hoyt, Kendall, and Stephen Brooks. 2003–4. "A Double-Edged Sword: Globalization and Biosecurity." *International Security* 28 (Winter): 123–48.

Hughes, David, Sandra Anderson, Sylvia Gerritsma, Kalsum Yusah, David Mayntz, Nigel Hywel-Jones, Johan Billen, and Jacobus Boomsma. 2009. "The Life of a Dead Ant: The Expression of an Adaptive Extended Phenotype." *American Naturalist* 174 (September): 424–33.

Hughes, David, Torsten Wappler, and Conrad Labandeira. 2010, August 18. "Ancient Death-Grip Leaf Scars Reveal Ant-Fungal Parasitism." *Biology Letters* 7: 67–70, doi:10.1098/rsbl.2010.0521.

Hughes, James. 2007. "The Chechnya Conflict: Freedom Fighters or Terrorists?" *Demokratizatsiya: The Journal of Post-Soviet Democratization* 15 (Summer): 293–311.

Hulsman, John, and A. Wess Mitchell. 2009. *The Godfather Doctrine: A Foreign Policy Parable*. Princeton, NJ: Princeton University Press.

Ikenberry, G. John. 2000. *After Victory*. Princeton, NJ: Princeton University Press.

Jackson, Patrick Thaddeus, and Daniel Nexon. 2009. "Paradigmatic Faults in International Relations Theory." *International Studies Quarterly* 53 (December): 907–30.

Jakobson, Linda, and Dean Knox. 2010, September. *New Foreign Policy Actors in China*. SIPRI Policy Paper 26. Stockholm: Stockholm International Peace Research Institute.

Janis, Irving. 1972. *Victims of Groupthink: A Psychological Study of Foreign-Policy Decisions and Fiascoes*. Boston: Houghton Mifflin.

Jervis, Robert. 1976. *Perception and Misperception in International Politics*. Princeton, NJ: Princeton University Press.

————. 1978. "Cooperation under the Security Dilemma." *World Politics* 30 (January): 167–214.

————. 1992. "Political Implications of Loss Aversion." *Political Psychology* 13 (June): 187–204.

Johnston, A. Iain. 2001. "Treating International Institutions as Social Environments." *International Studies Quarterly* 45 (December): 487–515.

Kagan, Donald, and Frederick Kagan. 2000. *While America Sleeps: Self-Delusion, Military Weakness, and the Threat to Peace Today*. New York: St. Martin's.

Kagan, Robert. 2003. *Of Paradise and Power: America and Europe in the New World Order*. New York: Alfred A. Knopf.

————. 2008. *The Return of History and the End of Dreams*. New York: Alfred A. Knopf.

Kahler, Miles, ed. 2009. *Networked Politics: Agency, Power, and Governance*. Ithaca, NY: Cornell University Press.

Kahn, Matthew. 2005. "The Death Toll from Natural Disasters: The Role of Income, Geography, and Institutions." *Review of Economics and Statistics* 87 (May): 271–84.

Kahneman, Daniel, and Jonathan Renshon. 2007. "Why Hawks Win." *Foreign Policy* 158 (January–February): 34–39.

Kahneman, Daniel, and Amos Tversky. 1979. "Prospect Theory: An Analysis of Decision under Risk." *Econometrica* 47 (March): 263–91.

Katzenstein, Peter, and Nobuo Okawara. 2001–2. "Japan, Asian-Pacific Security, and the Case for Analytical Eclecticism." *International Security* 26 (Winter): 153–85.

Kaufmann, Chaim. 2004. "Threat Inflation and the Failure of the Marketplace of Ideas: The Selling of the Iraq War," *International Security* 29 (Summer): 5–48.

Kay, Glenn. 2008. *Zombie Movies: The Ultimate Guide*. Chicago: Chicago Review Press.

Keck, Margaret, and Kathryn Sikkink. 1998. *Activists beyond Borders: Advocacy Networks in International Politics*. Ithaca, NY: Cornell University Press.

Keene, Brian. 2004. *The Rising*. New York: Leisure Books.

————. 2005. *City of the Dead*. New York: Delirium.

Kennan, George. 1984. *American Diplomacy*. Expanded ed. Chicago: University of Chicago Press.

Kennedy, Paul. 1987. *Rise and Fall of the Great Powers*. New York: Random House.

Keohane, Robert. 1984. *After Hegemony*. Princeton, NJ: Princeton University Press.

———. 1998. "Beyond Dichotomy: Conversations between International Relations and Feminist Theory." *International Studies Quarterly* 42 (March): 193–97.

Keohane, Robert, and Joseph Nye. 1978. *Power and Interdependence*. Boston: Scott Foresman.

Khan, Ali S. 2011, May 16. "Preparedness 101: Zombie Apocalypse." *Public Health Matters* (blog), http://blogs.cdc.gov/publichealthmatters/2011/05/preparedness-101-zombie-apocalypse/. Accessed April 5, 2014.

Khong, Yuen Foong. 1992. *Analogies at War*. Princeton, NJ: Princeton University Press.

Kiersey, Nicholas, and Iver Neumann, eds. 2013. Battlestar Galactica *and International Relations*. London: Routledge.

Kim, Woosang. 1992. "Power Transitions and Great Power War from Westphalia to Waterloo." *World Politics* 45 (October): 153–72.

Kimball, Ann Marie. 2006. *Risky Trade: Infectious Disease in the Era of Global Trade*. Aldershot, England: Ashgate.

King, Gary, Robert Keohane, and Sidney Verba. 1994. *Designing Social Inquiry*. Princeton, NJ: Princeton University Press.

King, Stephen. 2006. *Cell*. New York: Charles Scribner's Sons.

Klotz, Lynn, and Edward Sylvester. 2009. *Breeding Bio Insecurity: How U.S. Biodefense is Exporting Fear, Globalizing Risk, and Making Us All Less Secure*. Chicago: University of Chicago Press.

Knobler, Stanley, Adel Mahmoud, and Stanley Lemon, eds. 2006. *The Impact of Globalization on Infectious Disease Emergence and Control: Exploring the Consequences and Opportunities*. Washington, DC: National Academies Press.

Koblentz, Gregory. 2010. "Biosecurity Reconsidered: Calibrating Biological Threats and Responses." *International Security* 34 (Spring): 96–132.

Koch, Christof, and Francis Crick. 2001. "On the Zombie Within." *Nature* 411 (June): 893.

Kohut, Andrew, and Bruce Stokes. 2006. *America against the World*. New York: Times Books.

Krasner, Stephen D. 1991. "Global Communications and National Power: Life on the Pareto Frontier." *World Politics* 43 (April): 336–66.

Krauthammer, Charles. 2004. *Democratic Realism: An American Foreign Policy for a Unipolar World*. Washington, DC: American Enterprise Institute.

Kristol, Irving. 1983. *Reflections of a Neoconservative*. New York: Basic Books.

Kristol, William, and David Brooks. 1997, September 15. "What Ails Conservatism." *Wall Street Journal*.

Kristol, William, and Robert Kagan. 1996. "Towards a Neo-Reaganite Foreign Policy." *Foreign Affairs* 75 (July–August): 18–32.

———, eds. 2000. *Present Dangers: Crisis and Opportunity in American Foreign and Defense Policy*. San Francisco: Encounter.

Krasner, Stephen D. 1978. *Defending the National Interest: Raw Materials Investment and U.S. Foreign Policy*. Princeton, NJ: Princeton University Press.

Krugman, Paul. 2013, February 14. "Rubio and the Zombies." *New York Times*.

Lake, David. 2001. "Beyond Anarchy: The Importance of Security Institutions." *International Security* 26 (Summer): 129–60.

———. 2011. "Why 'Isms' Are Evil: Theory, Epistemology, and Academic Sects as Impediments to Understanding and Progress." *International Studies Quarterly* 55 (March): 465–80.

LaPierre, Wayne. 2013, February 2. "Stand and Fight." *Daily Caller*, http://dailycaller.com/2013/02/13/stand-and-fight/. Accessed April 4, 2014.

Lauro, Sarah Juliet, and Karen Embry. 2008. "A Zombie Manifesto: The Nonhuman Condition in the Era of Advanced Capitalism." *Boundary* 2 (Spring): 85–108.

Lazer, David. 2011. "Networks in Political Science: Back to the Future." *PS: Political Science and Politics* 44 (March): 61–68.

Legro, Jeffrey, and Andrew Moravcsik. 1999. "Is Anyone Still a Realist?" *International Security* 24 (Spring): 55–106.

Levin, Josh. 2004, March 24. "Dead Run: How Did Zombies Get so Fast?" *Slate*, http://www.slate.com/id/2097751. Accessed July 15, 2010.

Levy, Jack. 1997. "Prospect Theory, Rational Choice, and International Relations." *International Studies Quarterly* 41 (March): 87–112.

Li, Cheng. 2009. "China's Team of Rivals." *Foreign Policy* 171 (March–April): 88–93.

Lipson, Charles. 1984. "International Cooperation in Economic and Security Affairs," *World Politics* 37 (October): 1–23.

Littlewood, Roland, and Chavannes Douyon. 1997. "Clinical Findings in Three Cases of Zombification." *Lancet* 350 (October 11): 1094–96.

Loudermilk, A. 2003. "Eating 'Dawn' in the Dark: Zombie Desire and Commodified Identity in George A. Romero's 'Dawn of the Dead.'" *Journal of Consumer Culture* 3 (March): 83–108.

Louison, Cole, ed. 2009. *U.S. Army Zombie Combat Skills*. Guilford, CT: Lyons.

Ma, Roger. 2010. *The Zombie Combat Manual: A Guide to Fighting the Living Dead*. New York: Berkley.

Maberry, Jonathan. 2008. *Zombie CSU: The Forensics of the Living Dead*. New York: Citadel.

Maliniak, Daniel, Ryan M. Powers, and Barbara F. Walter. 2013. "The Gender Citation Gap in International Relations." *International Organization* 67, doi: 10.1017/S0020818313000209.

Marion, Isaac. 2011. *Warm Bodies*. New York: Atria.

Markovsky, Barry, and Shane Thye. 2001. "Social Influence on Paranormal Beliefs." *Sociological Perspectives* 44 (Spring): 21–44.

Marlin-Bennett, Renée, Marieke Wilson, and Jason Walton. 2010. "Commodified Cadavers and the Political Economy of the Spectacle." *International Political Sociology* 4 (June): 159–77.

Martin, Lisa. 1992. *Coercive Cooperation: Explaining Multilateral Economic Sanctions*. Princeton, NJ: Princeton University Press.

———. 2000. *Democratic Commitments: Legislatures and International Cooperation*. Stanford, CA: Stanford University Press.

Mastanduno, Michael. 1992. *Economic Containment: COCOM and the Politics of East-West Trade*. Ithaca, NY: Cornell University Press.

McNeill, William. 1976. *Plagues and Peoples*. New York: Anchor.

Mearsheimer, John. 2001. *The Tragedy of Great Power Politics*. New York: W. W. Norton.

Mearsheimer, John, and Stephen Walt. 2007. *The Israel Lobby and U.S. Foreign Policy*. New York: Farrar, Straus and Giroux.

Mercer, Jonathan. 1995. "Anarchy and Identity." *International Organization* 49 (March): 229–52.

———. 1996. *Reputation and International Politics*. Ithaca, NY: Cornell University Press.

Messer, Blake. 2010, March 10. "Agent-Based Computational Model of Humanity's Prospects for Post Zombie Outbreak Survival." *The Tortoise's Lens* (blog), http://the tortoiseslens.blogspot.com/2010/03/agent-based-computational-model-of.html. Accessed July 15, 2010.

Milner, Helen. 1997. *Interests, Institutions, and Information: Domestic Politics and International Relations*. Princeton, NJ: Princeton University Press.

Mitchell, Jerry, Deborah Thomas, Arleen Hill, and Susan Cutter. 2000. "Catastrophe in Reel Life versus Real Life: Perpetuating Disaster Myth through Hollywood Films."

International Journal of Mass Emergencies and Disasters 18 (November): 383–402.

Mitzen, Jennifer. 2006. "Ontological Security in World Politics: State Identity and the Security Dilemma." *European Journal of International Relations* 12 (September): 341–70.

Moe, Terry. 1990. "The Politics of Structural Choice: Towards a Theory of Public Bureaucracy." In *Organization Theory*, ed. Oliver Williamson, 116–53. New York: Oxford University Press.

Moïsi, Dominique. 2007. "The Clash of Emotions." *Foreign Affairs* 86 (January–February): 8–12.

Molloy, Patricia. 2003. "Demon Diasporas: Confronting the Other and the Other Worldly in *Buffy the Vampire Slayer* and *Angel*." In *To Seek Out New Worlds: Science Fiction and World Politics*, ed. Jutta Weldes, 99–121. New York: Palgrave Macmillan.

Moody, Todd. 1994. "Conversations with Zombies." *Journal of Consciousness Studies* 1 (February): 196–200.

Moon, Katharine Hyung-Sun. 1997. *Sex among Allies: Military Prostitution in U.S.-Korea Relations*. New York: Columbia University Press.

Moravcsik, Andrew. 1997. "Taking Preferences Seriously: A Liberal Theory of International Politics," *International Organization* 51 (Autumn): 513–53.

Morgenthau, Hans. 1948. *Politics among Nations*. New York: McGraw-Hill.

Mori, Masahiro. 1970. "The Uncanny Valley." *Energy* 7 (December): 33–35.

Most, Benjamin, and Harvey Starr. 1984. "International Relations Theory, Foreign Policy Substitutability, and 'Nice' Laws." *World Politics* 36 (April): 383–406.

Mueller, John. 2009a. *Atomic Obsession: Nuclear Alarmism from Hiroshima to al-Qaeda*. New York: Oxford University Press.

———. 2009b. "War Has Almost Ceased to Exist: An Assessment." *Political Science Quarterly* 124 (Spring): 297–321.

Muller, Benjamin. 2008. "Securing the Political Imagination: Popular Culture, the Security Dispositif and the Biometric State." *Security Dialogue* 39 (April): 199–220.

Murphy, Craig N. 1996. "Seeing Women, Recognizing Gender, Recasting International Relations." *International Organization* 50 (Summer): 513–38.

Nadelmann, Ethan. 1990. "Global Prohibition Regimes: The Evolution of Norms in International Society." *International Organization* 44 (Autumn): 479–526.

Naim, Moises. 2013. *The End of Power: From Boardrooms to Battlefields and Churches to States, Why Being In Charge Isn't What It Used to Be.* New York: Basic Books.

Nel, Philip, and Marjolein Righarts. 2008. "Natural Disasters and the Risk of Violent Conflict." *International Studies Quarterly* 52 (March): 159–85.

Neustadt, Richard, and Earnest May. 1986. *Thinking in Time: The Uses of History for Decision-Makers.* New York: Simon and Schuster.

Newitz, Analee. 2006. *Pretend We're Dead: Capitalist Monsters in American Pop Culture.* Durham, NC: Duke University Press.

———. 2008, October 29. "War and Social Upheaval Cause Spikes in Zombie Movie Production." *io9* (blog), http://io9.com/5070243/war-and-social-upheaval-cause-spikes-in-zombie-movie-production. Accessed September 15, 2010.

Nexon, Daniel, and Iver Neumann, eds. 2006. *Harry Potter and International Relations.* New York: Rowman and Littlefield.

Nicolaides, Christos, Luis Cueto-Felgueroso, and Ruben Juanes. 2013. "The Price of Anarchy in Mobility-Driven Contagion Dynamics." *Journal of the Royal Society Interface* 10: 1–11.

Nye, Joseph. 2004. *Soft Power: The Means to Success in World Politics.* New York: Public Affairs.

Oatley, Thomas, W. Kindred Winecoff, Andrew Pennock, and Sarah Bauerle Danzman. 2013. "The Political Economy of Global Finance: A Network Model." *Perspectives on Politics* 11 (March): 133–53.

Ó Gráda, Cormac. 2009. *Famine: A Short History*. Princeton, NJ: Princeton University Press.

Oatley, Thomas, W. Kindred Winecoff, Andrew Pennock, and Sarah Bauerle Danzman. 2013. "The Political Economy of Global Finance: A Network Model." *Perspectives on Politics* 11 (March): 133–53.

Olson, Mancur. 1971. *The Logic of Collective Action: Public Goods and the Theory of Groups*. Cambridge, MA: Harvard University Press.

Organski, A.F.K. 1958. *World Politics*. New York: Alfred A. Knopf.

Ornstein, Norman, and Thomas Mann. 2006. "When Congress Checks Out," *Foreign Affairs* 85 (November–December): 67–82.

Paffenroth, Kim. 2006. *Gospel of the Living Dead: George Romero's Visions of Hell on Earth*. Houston, TX: Baylor University Press.

Paris, Roland. 2001. "Human Security: Paradigm Shift or Hot Air?" *International Security* 26 (Fall): 87–102.

Perrow, Charles. *Normal Accidents*. New York: Basic Books.

Peterson, V. Spike. 1992. "Transgressing Boundaries: Theories of Knowledge, Gender and International Relations." *Millennium* 21 (Spring): 183–206.

Pew Research Center. 2009. *America's Place in the World 2009*, http://www.people-press.org/files/legacy-pdf/569.pdf. Accessed April 25, 2014.

———. 2013. *America's Place in the World 2009*, http://www.people-press.org/files/legacy-pdf/12-3-2013%20APW%20VI.pdf. Accessed April 25, 2014.

Phelan, Chanda. 2009. "Omega-Alpha." Bachelor's thesis, Department of English, Pomona College, Claremont, CA.

Phillips, Erica. 2014, March 3. "Zombie Studies Gain Ground on College Campuses." *Wall Street Journal*.

Pinker, Steven. 2011. *The Better Angels of Our Nature: Why Violence Has Declined*. New York: Viking.

Podhoretz, Norman. 2007. *World War IV: The Long Struggle against Islamofascism*. New York: Doubleday.

Powell, Robert. 1991. "Absolute and Relative Gains in International Relations Theory." *American Political Science Review* 85 (December): 1303–20.

Price-Smith, Andrew. 2002. *The Health of Nations: Infectious Disease, Environmental Change, and Their Effects on National Security and Development.* Cambridge, MA: MIT Press.

Przeworski, Adam, and Michael Wallerstein. 1988. "Structural Dependence of the State on Capital," *American Political Science Review* 82 (February): 11–29.

Putnam, Robert. 1988. "Diplomacy and Domestic Politics: The Logic of Two-Level Games." *International Organization* 42 (Summer): 427–60.

Quarantelli, E. L. 2004. "Sociology of Panic." In *International Encyclopedia of the Social and Behavioral Sciences,* ed. Neal Smelser and Paul Baltes, 11020–30. New York: Elsevier.

Quiggin, John. 2010. *Zombie Economics.* Princeton, NJ: Princeton University Press.

Rapport, Aaron. 2008. "Unexpected Affinities? Neoconservatism's Place in IR Theory." *Security Studies* 17 (April): 257–93.

Raustiala, Kal, and David Victor. 2004. "The Regime Complex for Plant Genetic Resources." *International Organization* 58 (Spring): 277–309.

Recht, Z. A. 2006. *Plague of the Dead.* New York: Permuted Press.

Risse-Kappen, Thomas. 1991. "Public Opinion, Domestic Structure, and Foreign Policy in Liberal Democracies." *World Politics* 43 (July): 479–512.

Rose, Gideon. 1998. "Neoclassical Realism and Theories of Foreign Policy." *World Politics* 51 (October): 144–72.

Rossman, Gabriel. 2010, March 12. "Fiddler's Green." *Code and Culture: Stata, Sociology and Diffusion Models* (blog), http://codeandculture.wordpress.com/2010/03/12/fiddlers-green/. Accessed July 15, 2010.

Ruane, Abigail, and Patrick James. 2008. "The International Relations of Middle-Earth: Learning from *The*

Lord of the Rings." *International Studies Perspectives* 9 (November): 377–94.

Rudolph, Volker, and Janis Antonovics. 2007. "Disease Transmission by Cannibalism: Rare Event or Common Occurrence?" *Proceedings of the Royal Society* 274 (February): 1205–10.

Russell, Jamie. 2005. *Book of the Dead: The Complete History of Zombie Cinema.* Surrey, England: FAB.

Russett, Bruce, and John Oneal. 1997. "The Classical Liberals Were Right: Democracy, Interdependence, and Conflict, 1950–1985." *International Studies Quarterly* 41 (June): 267–93.

Schlozman, Steven. 2011. *The Zombie Autopsies: Secret Notebooks from the Apocalypse.* Boston: Grand Central.

Schweller, Randall. 2010. "Entropy and the Trajectory of World Politics: Why Polarity Has Become Less Meaningful." *Cambridge Journal of International Affairs* 23 (March): 145–63.

Sell, Susan. 2003. *Private Power, Public Law: The Globalization of Intellectual Property Rights.* Cambridge: Cambridge University Press.

Sen, Amartya. 1983. *Poverty and Famines: An Essay on Entitlement and Deprivation.* Oxford: Oxford University Press.

Sil, Rudra, and Peter Katzenstein. 2010. "Analytic Eclecticism in the Study of World Politics." *Perspectives on Politics* 8 (June): 411–31.

Simmons, Beth. 2009. *Mobilizing for Human Rights: International Law in Domestic Politics.* New York: Cambridge University Press.

Simon, Herbert. 1976. *Administrative Behavior.* 3rd ed. New York: Free Press.

Sjoberg, Laura, and Caron E. Gentry. 2007. *Mothers, Monsters, Whores: Women's Violence in Global Politics.* London: Zed.

Slaughter, Anne-Marie. 2004. *A New World Order.* Princeton, NJ: Princeton University Press.

———. 2009. "America's Edge: Power in the Networked Century." *Foreign Affairs* 88 (January–February): 94–113.

Smith?, Robert J., ed. 2011. *BRAAAIIINNNSSS! From Academic to Zombies*. Ottawa, Ontario, Canada: University of Ottawa Press.

Smith?, Robert J., Philip Munz, Ioan Hudea, and Joe Imad. 2009. "When Zombies Attack! Mathematical Modelling of an Outbreak of a Zombie Infection." In *Infectious Disease: Modelling Research Progress*, ed. Jean Michel Tcheunche and Christinah Chiyaka, 133–50. Hauppauge, NY: Nova Science.

Snidal, Duncan. 1985. "The Game Theory of International Politics." *World Politics* 38 (October): 25–57.

———. 1991. "Relative Gains and the Pattern of International Cooperation." *American Political Science Review* 85 (September): 701–26.

Snower, Dennis. 1982. "Macroeconomic Policy and the Optimal Destruction of Vampires." *Journal of Political Economy* 90 (June): 647–55.

Snyder, Jack. 1991. *Myths of Empire*. Ithaca, NY: Cornell University Press.

———. 2002. "Anarchy and Culture: Insights from the Anthropology of War." *International Organization* 56 (Winter): 7–45.

Solnit, Rebecca. 2009. *A Paradise Built in Hell: The Extraordinary Communities That Arise in Disaster*. New York: Viking.

Sparks, Glenn, C. Leigh Nelson, and Rose Campbell. 1997. "The Relationship between Exposure to Televised Messages about Paranormal Phenomena and Paranormal Beliefs." *Journal of Broadcasting and Electronic Media* 41 (Summer): 345–59.

Stanger, Allison. 2009. *One Nation under Contract: The Outsourcing of American Power and the Future of Foreign Policy*. New Haven, CT: Yale University Press.

Steans, Jill. 1998. *Gender and International Relations: An Introduction*. New Brunswick, NJ: Rutgers University Press.

Stern, Jessica. 2002–3. "Dreaded Risks and the Control of Biological Weapons." *International Security* 27 (Winter): 89–123.

Strong, Philip. 1990. "Epidemic Psychology: A Model." *Sociology of Health and Illness* 12 (September): 249–59.

Sunstein, Cass, and Adrian Vermeule. 2008. *Conspiracy Theories*. Law and Economics Research Paper Series 387. Chicago: University of Chicago Law School.

Suskind, Ron. 2004, October 17. "Faith, Certainty, and the Presidency of George W. Bush." *New York Times Magazine*.

———. 2006. *The One Percent Doctrine: Deep inside America's Pursuit of Its Enemies Since 9/11*. New York: Simon and Schuster.

Sylvester, Christine. 2002. *Feminist International Relations: An Unfinished Journey*. Cambridge: Cambridge University Press.

———. 2013. "Experiencing the End and Afterlives of International Relations/Theory." *European Journal of International Relations* 19 (September): 609–26.

Tannenwald, Nina. 1999. "The Nuclear Taboo: The United States and the Normative Basis of Nuclear Non-Use." *International Organization* 53 (July): 433–68.

———. 2005. "Stigmatizing the Bomb: Origins of the Nuclear Taboo." *International Security* 29 (Spring): 5–49.

Tetlock, Philip. 2005. *Expert Political Judgment*. Princeton, NJ: Princeton University Press.

Thaler, Richard, and Cass Sunstein. 2008. *Nudge: Improving Decisions about Health, Wealth and Happiness*. New Haven, CT: Yale University Press.

Tickner, J. Ann. 1992. *Gender in International Relations: Feminist Perspectives on Achieving Global Security*. New York: Columbia University Press.

———. 1997. "You Just Don't Understand: Troubled Engagements between Feminists and IR Theorists." *International Studies Quarterly* 41 (December): 611–32.

Tickner, J. Ann, and Laura Sjoberg. 2013. "Feminism." in *International Relations Theories: Discipline and Diversity*, 3rd ed., ed. Steve Smith, Tim Dunne, and Milja Kurki, 195–212. Oxford: Oxford University Press.

Tierney, Kathleen. 2004, January 30. "Collective Behavior in Times of Crisis." Paper presented at the National Research Council Roundtable on Social and Behavioral Sciences and Terrorism, National Academies, Washington, DC.

Tierney, Kathleen, Christine Bevc, and Erica Kuligowski. 2006. "Metaphors Matter: Disaster Myths, Media Frames, and their Consequences in Hurricane Katrina." *Annals of the American Academy of Political and Social Science* 604 (March): 57–81.

Twain, Mark, and W. Bill Czolgosz. 2009. *Adventures of Huckleberry Finn and Zombie Jim*. Winnipeg, Manitoba, Canada: Coscom.

Twitchell, James. 1985. *Dreadful Pleasures: An Anatomy of Modern Horror*. New York: Oxford University Press.

Twohy, Margaret. 2008. "From Voodoo to Viruses: The Evolution of the Zombie in Twentieth Century Popular Culture." Master's thesis, Trinity College Dublin.

United States Strategic Command. 2011. CONPLAN 8888–11: Counter-Zombie Dominance. Accessed at http://i2.cdn.turner.com/cnn/2014/images/05/16/dod.zombie.apocalypse.plan.pdf, June 2014.

Van Belle, Douglas. 1998. "Balance of Power and System Stability: Simulating Complex Anarchical Environments over the Internet," *Political Research Quarterly* 51 (March): 265–82.

Van Belle, Douglas, Kenneth Mash, and Joseph Braunwarth. 2010. *A Novel Approach to Politics*. 2nd ed. Washington: CQ.

VanDusky, Julie. 2010, November 20. "BRAINZ! . . . Zombie Movies and War, An Odd Correlation." *The Quantitative Peace* (blog), http://www.quantitativepeace.com/blog/2008/11/brainz-zombie-movies-and-war-an-odd-correlation.html. Accessed September 15, 2010.

Vass, Arpad. 2001. "Beyond the Grave—Understanding Human Decomposition." *Microbiology Today* 28 (November): 190–92.

Waldmann, Paul. 2009, June 16. "The Left and the Living Dead." *American Prospect*, http://www.prospect.org/cs/

articles?article=the_left_and_the_living_dead. Accessed July 15, 2010.

Walker, Thomas C. 2010. "The Perils of Paradigm Mentalities: Revisiting Kuhn, Lakatos, and Popper." *Perspectives on Politics* 8 (June): 433–51.

Wallace, Jeremy. 2011. "Authoritarian Information Problems: Data Manipulation in China." Unpublished manuscript, Ohio State University.

Waller, Gregory. 2010. *The Living and the Undead: Slaying Vampires, Exterminating Zombies*. Champaign: University of Illinois Press.

Walt, Stephen M. 1987. *The Origins of Alliances*. Ithaca, NY: Cornell University Press.

———. 1996. *Revolution and War*. Ithaca, NY: Cornell University Press.

———. 2005. *Taming American Power*. New York: W.W. Norton.

Waltz, Kenneth N. 1959. *Man, the State and War: A Theoretical Analysis*. New York: Columbia University Press.

———. 1979. *Theory of International Politics*. New York: McGraw Hill.

Ward, Michael D., Katherine Stovel, and Audrey Sacks. 2011. "Network Analysis and Political Science." *Annual Review of Political Science* 14: 245–64.

Waters, Jennifer Hardison, Andrew Moore, Marcus Berzofsky, and Lynn Langton. 2013. *Household Burglary, 1994–2011*. Bureau of Justice Statistics report NCJ 241754, http://www.bjs.gov/contentpub/pdf/hb9411.pdf. Accessed April 23, 2014.

Webb, Jen, and Sam Byrnard. 2008. "Some Kind of Virus: The Zombie as Body and as Trope." *Body and Society* 14 (June): 83–98.

Weber, Cynthia. 2006. *Imagining America at War: Morality, Politics and Film*. London: Routledge.

Weeks, Jessica. 2008. "Autocratic Audience Costs: Regime Type and Signaling Resolve." *International Organization* 62 (January): 35–64.

Weingast, Barry, and Mark Moran. 1983. "Bureaucratic Discretion of Congressional Control: Regulatory Policymaking by the Federal Trade Commission." *Journal of Political Economy* 91 (October): 765–800.

Weinstein, Neil. 1980. "Unrealistic Optimism about Future Life Events." *Journal of Personality and Social Psychology* 39 (May): 806–20.

Weldes, Jutta, ed. 2003. *To Seek Out New Worlds: Science Fiction and World Politics*. New York: Palgrave Macmillan.

Wellington, David. 2006a. *Monster Island*. New York: Thunder's Mouth.

———. 2006b. *Monster Nation*. New York: Running Press.

———. 2007. *Monster Planet*. New York: Running Press.

Wendt, Alexander. 1999. *Social Theory of International Politics*. New York: Cambridge University Press.

———. 2003. "Why a World State Is Inevitable." *European Journal of International Relations* 9 (December): 491–542.

Wendt, Alexander, and Raymond Duvall. 2008. "Sovereignty and the UFO." *Political Theory* 36 (August): 607–33.

Wexler, Laura. 2008, April 13. "Commando Performance." *Washington Post*.

Whitehead, Colson. 2011. *Zone One*. New York: Doubleday.

Whitman, Glen, and James Dow, eds. 2014. *Economics of the Undead: Blood, Brains, and Benjamins*. New York: Rowman and Littlefield.

Wilentz, Amy. 2012, October 30. "A Zombie Is a Slave Forever." *New York Times*.

Williams, Michael. 2005. "What Is the National Interest? The Neoconservative Challenge in IR Theory." *European Journal of International Relations* 11 (September): 307–37.

Wilson, Craig. 2009, April 10. "Zombies Lurch into Popular Culture via Books, Plays, More." *USA Today*.

Wilson, James Q. 1989. *Bureaucracy: What Government Agencies Do and Why They Do It*. New York: Basic Books.

Wilson, Meagan Meuchel. 2014. *Hate Crime Victimization, 2004–2012: Statistical Table*. Bureau of Justice Statistics report NCJ 244409, http://www.bjs.gov/content/pub/pdf/hcvo412st.pdf. Accessed April 23, 2014.

Woerner, Meredith. 2012, November 28. "And Now, a Reading from the Best Undead Novel of Our Time: *Z Is for Zombie*." *io9* (blog), http://io9.com/5964126/and-now-a-reading-from-the-best-undead-novel-of-our-time-z-is-for-zombie. Accessed April 4, 2014.

Yglesias, Matthew. 2014. "The Good News About Gun Violence in America." *Vox*, http://www.vox.com/2014/5/25/5749316/us-murder-rate-decline, accessed June 27, 2014.

Youde, Jeremy. 2012. "Biosurveillance, Human Rights, and the Zombie Plague." *Global Change, Peace and Security* 24 (January): 83–93.

Zakaraia, Fareed. 1998. *From Wealth to Power: The Unusual Origins of America's World Role*. Princeton, NJ: Princeton University Press.

Zalewski, Marysia, and Anne Sisson Runyan. 2013. "Taking Feminist Violence Seriously in Feminist International Relations." *International Feminist Journal of Politics* 15 (Summer): 293–313.

Zenko, Micah, and Michael Cohen. 2012. "Clear and Present Safety." *Foreign Affairs* 91 (March–April): 79–91.

Zegart, Amy. 2007. *Spying Blind: The CIA, the FBI, and the Origins of 9/11*. Princeton, NJ: Princeton University Press.

INDEX